AGENTS OF CHANGE

RETHINKING INSURANCE AGENCY MARKETING

John M. Tate
Jay Adkins
Natalia Tate

Copyright © 2017 Agency Marketing Machine, LLC

Published by Hyndsight 20/20
ISBN-13: 978-0692841044
ISBN-10: 0692841040

DEDICATION

We dedicate this book to our Agency Marketing Machine clients - the hometown insurance agencies across the country who understood that they needed to do things differently and embraced our concepts. Thank you from the bottom of our hearts for providing further proof that doing the right things is also the best thing for business.

A big thank you to Stephanie Hynds for contributing her special talents to this project, and to the rest of our dedicated and creative team at AMM. The passion and energy you pour into driving our clients' achievements each and every day brings us great joy.

ACKNOWLEDGEMENT

"Our textbooks should not present us with a series of end results but rather a plot that enables the reader to go through the deduction process himself."

-Eliyahu M. Goldratt, author of "The Goal", which was a significant influence on both the format for this book and its authors

CONTENTS

FOREWARD 1

CHAPTER ONE *WHEN YOUR BEST JUST ISN'T GOOD ENOUGH*.............. 3

CHAPTER TWO *OH, WHAT A TANGLED WEB WE WEAVE* 10

CHAPTER THREE *AND THE HITS JUST KEEP ON COMING*...................23

CHAPTER FOUR *WE REACH CRITICAL MASS*......................................39

CHAPTER FIVE *IS THAT A LIGHT AT THE END OF THE TUNNEL OR JUST AN ONCOMING TRAIN?*..58

CHAPTER SIX *WHAT GOES AROUND, COMES AROUND* 72

CHAPTER SEVEN *TO BE OR NOT TO BE A SOCIAL BUTTERFLY*..........88

CHAPTER EIGHT *THE IMMORTAL WORDS OF P.T. BARNUM* 101

CHAPTER NINE *IT'S A VOLUNTARY THING* 114

CHAPTER TEN *SOMETHING FROM NOTHING* 129

CHAPTER ELEVEN *LIGHTS, CAMERA, ACTION!*................................. 144

CHAPTER TWELVE *AGENTS OF CHANGE* 158

EPILOGUE.. 167

FOREWARD

Each chapter in this book is divided into two distinct sections.

The first section contains an ongoing story about Jim Wakefield, an insurance agency owner who must figure out a way to not only find more customers, but also learn how to retain them. This is a fictional story, but the tactics that Jim learns and implements are very real.

The second section of each chapter contains a more detailed review of exactly what Jim learned and the reasons why those tactics did, or didn't, work. This portion is written in our voice, the authors of this book... John, Jay and Natalia.

We also happen to be the founders of a company called Agency Marketing Machine.

Agency Marketing Machine operates as the marketing department for hundreds of insurance agencies across the nation. John (the marketing guy), Jay (the insurance guy) and Natalia (the PR gal) created the company to help local insurance agencies take advantage of the new digital tools available in our modern world today, and use them as the means to amplify the essential *truths of old*.

We're excited to guide you on Jim's journey as he discovers some of these tools, and comes to realize the impact of their proper usage. The research findings of Jim and his team are factual and footnoted, and matching results from his activities can be found in hundreds of individual successes that Agency Marketing Machine has helped to produce for our clients.

Also in the second section of each chapter, you'll be directed to free resources which will arm you with easy-to-use, detailed instructions and templates we think you'll find very helpful.

Although this book *can* be used as a marketing success template for every insurance agency, we know that it's *not* going to happen.

It won't happen simply because there are some things which may necessitate a change of culture, a change of habits, even a change of mindset. Above all, as with anything worthwhile, it will take some effort. Because, unfortunately, there are no silver bullets. And that fact will no doubt eliminate a very large percentage of agency owners from giving the activities proper attention, even if it means the death of the agency months or years away.

But those who do implement these strategies will have found a way to market their businesses that will stand the test of time... and they will truly become *Agents Of Change*.

Now, let's see what's going on with agency owner Jim Wakefield!

CHAPTER ONE
WHEN YOUR BEST JUST ISN'T GOOD ENOUGH

As I hang up the phone, I can't help but feel frustrated. Another customer has just dropped their insurance because they found a way to save money somewhere else. It's getting harder and harder to counter that objection when all customers seem to see anymore is price.

I sigh and push my chair away from my desk.

Unfortunately, keeping customers isn't the only seemingly insurmountable problem I'm facing right now. One of my highest producers left recently when her husband's employer transferred them to San Diego.

Happy Thanksgiving, Jim. Yeah, right. I sigh again.

But retaining customers and good staff isn't my only problem, or even the biggest one. The real problem is where do I find more? More clients, more good agents – people who will stay with my agency for longer than two weeks?

I'd been riding the roller coaster of buying leads, but the quality was so flat-out bad that I stopped. In hindsight, was that really the best decision? Yeah, it was expensive, but at least it made me feel like I was doing *something*. What the heck am I going to do now?

Disgusted, I leave for lunch, catching my staff off guard. I'm usually chained to my desk between 8:00 a.m. and 6:30 p.m., often later, and just taking off in the middle of the day is unheard of for me. But I desperately need to get some distance and think.

Are these problems I'm facing *actually* insurmountable? Or is there a way out that I'm just not seeing?

It's a typical January day in northeast Ohio – frigid, gray and blustery. Perfect. It matches my mood.

Striding from the door of the insurance and financial services firm that I purchased two years ago, I jump into my Jeep Grand Cherokee and drive aimlessly for a few minutes. For the first time, I really look at the strip malls and other buildings I pass. Wow. So many abandoned, empty and for rent.

Geez, an awful lot of businesses seem to be going under. Could that happen to me? Surely not. Surely a reasonably intelligent person can figure a way out of this thorny predicament, no matter how thorny it may seem.

Parking my car and ducking into a sandwich shop, I sit and place my order, completely distracted.

I come from such a structured environment. Working for the school system as a high school physics teacher was terrific security and a regular paycheck. And the hours were great. But although I loved teaching, after fifteen years I felt like I was stagnating; like there had to be more to life.

That was when I first read 'Rich Dad, Poor Dad', and everything changed. I finally realized what my true dream was – owning my own business. My wife Cindy had supported me 100% and we put ourselves on a tight budget and began saving like crazy.

It took several years, but when we had finally saved up enough money to take the plunge, things just sort of fell into place, as if it was all meant to be. My buddy knew an agent who was retiring and selling his insurance business and it seemed like a perfect fit. I had always enjoyed taking care of my students; now I could take care of my clients and keep them and their families protected.

I couldn't have been more excited to be my own man, the captain of my own ship. It felt like *freedom*.

Freedom? I snorted. I'd never felt so trapped in my life.

In fact, that teaching job was looking pretty cushy right about now. At least when I was there I never had to worry about making payroll. I hadn't had my employees' livelihood and their families' future security resting on my shoulders. The responsibility of it all makes me feel like I'm in a vise that keeps tightening.

I notice a pen sitting on top of a check from the now vacant table next to me. Ever since I was a kid, I had a habit of doodling any time I was either thinking about something intently, lost in a sea of thoughts, or not thinking about too much at all.

My wife thinks my doodling serves as a sort of therapy, where all my negative thoughts and insecurities can be released, and then I can move on. Of course, since I'm not big on sharing my inner feelings – what guy is? – I try to keep my doodles away from prying eyes for the most part.

When I became a physics teacher, the stick figure that I always drew as me, suddenly began wearing a tie. Although I don't wear a tie in the insurance agency, my stick figure 'me,' for some reason, still wears one. Weird.

I removed the utensils from the napkin in front of me and made use of it.

I put down the pen and take a look at what I've absently doodled. Geez, powerlessness is a terrible feeling.

As I continue to sit and mull over all the problems in the state of my world today, I finally call the office and tell Mindy, one of two on my customer service team, that I won't be returning this afternoon. As she gasps and stutters, I hang up. Hey, man, I'm the boss. I can take a couple hours off if I want to, can't I? I hired Mindy right out of high school and she has zero filter on her communications. It keeps things loose in the office, which I like, but I'm really not in the mood for any of it today.

I continue to sit, lost in thought, losing all track of time.

Finally, I get up and drive home, where I find that Cindy has taken Kenzie, our 6 year old daughter, to indoor soccer practice. I know that I should join them, I get to spend so little time with them, but why spread around my lousy mood?

Anyway, Cindy will be mad at me whether I show up or not. She's been saying lately that even when I'm home, I'm so preoccupied that it's like I'm not even there. I know she's frustrated by the distance growing between us – hell, I am, *too* – but I just can't bring myself to tell her how bad things are at work.

It feels like failure. And she didn't sign up for that.

What if I just gave up and sold out?

Remembering all the boarded-up businesses I'd driven past today, I know that even if I could find a buyer, at this point I'd take a big loss. When I originally bought the agency and changed the name to Wakefield Insurance, we had lost a lot of customers – an old guard who was loyal to the previous owner.

If only I could find that kind of loyalty. Did it even exist anymore?

No, Jimbo, selling isn't the answer. It would not only push my retirement plans back for years, but Cindy and I might never recover financially. No. I simply *have* to find a way to make this work.

But how?

This is the part where the founders of Agency Marketing Machine will comment on Jim's problems and adventures. We'll provide further detail into why things are happening, and some guidance so that you may take immediate action, within your own agency, using any activities and solutions that work for Jim.

In years past, companies had a kind of built-in loyalty. Our worlds were small – a handful of blocks, a small town, a few thousand people. Places may have had only 1 or 2 car dealerships, realtors, lawyers, mechanics, insurance agents.

Our parents and grandparents knew everyone in town and patronized the same businesses for their entire lifetimes. They picked one and they stuck with it, year after year, even generation after generation, as folks handed their companies down to their children and families handed their loyalties down, as well.

No so much anymore.

Today, our population is constantly in transit. People move between cities and states regularly during their lifetimes. In fact, in 2014 more than 7.3 million people in the US moved between States.[1] The internet has taken us global, and made consumers much savvier.

Due to the internet, not only can people easily search to see all the agencies in their area, but they can choose to do business with

---

[1] 2014 US Census Bureau - State to State Migrations Table

a company that has no local office at all and handles everything online and by phone.

In addition, AMM's 2016 Insurance Industry Customer Survey[2] found that 16.6% of those surveyed would actively search for a new insurance agency if their monthly premium went up just $10.

Where's the loyalty?

The bottom line is that according to the Department of Labor, there are over 433,000 insurance agents in our nation vying for business.

Let's let that sink in for a minute.

433,000 insurance agents in the United States.

How the heck can Jim's agency, one small fish in a vast ocean of alternative options, possibly hope to stand out from the crowd?

Let's see if Jim can figure out how to overcome these overwhelming odds.

So grab a cup of coffee and pull up a chair.

We're in this *together* now.

---

[2] Insurance Industry Customer Survey - 2016. 1,019 responses analyzed from Survey Monkey Audience responses.

CHAPTER TWO
OH, WHAT A TANGLED WEB WE WEAVE

I head out early the next day, arriving at work by 6:30 a.m. I feel like I'm no closer to any answers, but am determined to come up with an Action Plan before the day gets going. Perhaps through divine inspiration? I left the house so early that Cindy was still in bed, and we barely had a chance to speak to each other last night.

As luck would have it, as soon as I get in I receive text messages from two different employees saying they've come down with the flu and will be out all day. *Shoot.* Must be the same flu that's ripping through Kenzie's school. All I can hope is that they'll be back tomorrow – and, of course, that I don't get it myself.

Meanwhile, the entire day has been derailed. Ah, the singular joys of being the boss. As Harry Truman once so famously said, "The buck stops here." Thanks a lot, Harry.

Any and all plans go out the window, along with my To-Do List, which I don't even have the opportunity to glance at all day. Customer service call after customer service call, I end the day feeling like I've spent close to 12 long hours simply treading water, without accomplishing a darn thing.

Cindy is reading Kenzie a story in bed when I get home, and curtly tells me there's a plate in the fridge I can heat up for dinner. As I bend to kiss her cheek, my wife turns her head away and continues with the story.

Guess I'm in trouble again.

Exhausted both physically and mentally, I reheat and eat my dinner at the kitchen table. Pushing my plate away, I pull over a legal pad, intending to finally draft my Action Plan. But over an hour later, I'm still sitting in front of a blank page, no closer to any solution.

As I move around the house turning out lights and locking up, I realize that Cindy and I have barely spoken a word to each other all day.

Again.

Sitting at my desk the next morning, I mull over the situation. First and foremost, I need to find another top producer while simultaneously creating more business so that once the new hire gets up to speed, the agency will have enough leads that he or she can make a good living. If they're able to earn well, maybe they'll stick around for awhile.

After I finish up my plan for hiring a new producer and post an ad for the position, I can now move on to developing a plan for generating more leads and writing more business.

And...Hmm...Nothing. Nada. Nein. Nyet. Zero. Zilch.

I sigh, looking down at my notepad. My constant doodling has taken over the page while I was lost in thought.

How can I possibly be so *clueless*?

Something clearly has to change. What is it exactly that I need to accomplish here? It *can't* be all about price; it can't be all about the commodity. Because sometimes I'll have the lowest rates and sometimes I won't.

So…how do I get people to focus on something *besides* price? What I need is to have my customers, instead of looking at the product, look at me and my agents, at the agency, and let us into their lives. They need to trust us. But how does that happen?

And like a lightning bolt, inspiration strikes.

What about Vince? He's supposed to be some kind of marketing whiz, isn't he? It's been a little while since we talked. I know I'll see him at our friend Kevin's wedding in a couple of months, but I need help now. And really, we've let way too much time go by as it is.

Kevin Kingston, Leonardo Vincenzo (Vince) and I became friends in college and have remained close, even though we don't get to see each other as much as we would like.

Vince lives out on the west coast and travels all the time, working as an expert consultant. Which is kind of funny, because although he's a real brainiac, a more laid-back, hippie/surfer-dude kind of guy you would never meet. Sort of an Owen Wilson type with a super-high IQ.

But Vince is the real deal and one of my oldest friends.

Having gone to school nearby, he has a few major clients in town and sort of a branch office, and is usually around for a few days every month. But we've both been so busy that it's been several months since our last visit.

Shoot, I lost my phone a few weeks ago and still haven't put all my numbers back in my new one. Hmm. Let me check my text messages. Ah, here we go. It should be in this string of texts here. Yup. There's area code 415 – San Francisco. Gotta be Vince.

I call immediately and get Vince's voicemail, per usual. "Hey, Vince, it's Jim! Sorry I missed you, buddy. I'm interested in picking your brain a little bit and was wondering if you were going to be in town anytime soon. Give me a call if you get a chance. It's been too long."

Towards the end of the day, my phone rings. It's Vince calling back.

"Jimbo! How's it hangin', man?"

"Hey, it's good to hear your voice, Vince! I'm hanging in there, how've you been?"

"Oh, you know me – perpetually on the move. As a matter of fact, I'm just finishing up some work in my hotel room before leaving for the airport. Time to go home and catch some waves! What can I do you for, my friend?"

I quickly begin to relate some of the staff problems I've been experiencing, my challenges in finding new business and even the ever-present questions about the appeal, or lack thereof, of my website.

Vince cuts me off. "Listen, I'm sitting here with my computer open. Let me jump on real quick and I'll take a peek at the website for you."

"Excellent. Go ahead and give it to me straight, Vince."

He spends a couple of minutes looking over the site while we chit chat a little, and finally says, "OK. What exactly are you trying to get at with your website, Jim?"

"What do you mean?"

"I mean, what story are you trying to tell your potential customer base? What does your business stand for? What are your values? How do you want to be thought of in the marketplace?"

"I want people to trust me with protecting them and their finances."

"Well, I'm sorry, buddy, but I'm not seeing anything of real value here. Sorry to be frank, but your website basically sucks. It doesn't tell me an engaging story – who you are, what you stand for. It really doesn't do anything to make me trust you or wanna do business with you."

He continues, "And it's very *old* looking, but not in a cool, retro way. The images are fuzzy and the content seems really dated. In the back of my mind, even if subconsciously, it'd make me think you aren't on top of the latest tools in the insurance and financial industry. And, man oh man, who designed your logo? Kenzie?"

"Ouch."

"Just callin' it like I see it, dude. But you know, that stuff is easy to fix. And that's where I'd start. You're one of the best guys I know, Jim. Make your brand show who you are and what you can do for people. Wish I had more time, but I gotta go, man. If I don't leave now, I'm gonna miss my plane."

I hang up the phone, deep in thought. Could this be the answer? A new logo; a new website? Present the world with a contemporary new face for the agency?

With a smile slowly spreading across my face, I begin making plans.

Ten weeks later, I sit down to review my brand spankin' new website's analytics. As an ex-physics teacher, I loooove me some data. And the numbers…man, oh man, numbers just don't lie. It's not like I really thought the new website would fix all my problems (although a guy can hope), but surely I should be seeing *some* calls and requests for quotes. And, granted, there have been a few. But only a few.

It seems that almost all the site visitors are from outside of the United States. Probably from spam and robots. Sheesh, you'd think after spending $6,000 on a new logo and website, I'd at least have *something* to show for it.

I shake my head. This was supposed to generate leads, for heaven's sake. What a bunch of bull!

In a moment of uncharacteristic anger, I fire off a frustrated text message to Vince.

'Thanks alot, Vince. I spent 6 grand on a new logo and website and am getting zip out of it!'

After a few minutes, Vince texts, 'Sorry, man. Websites aren't like a Field of Dreams, you know.'

I sputter. That's it?

I quickly send another text, 'No kidding. Well, I spent another $900 on Google ads in one month and got ZERO calls!'

A minute later the phone rings. It's Vince.

"Hey, Jim, pause your ad word campaign pronto. I'm sorry I never got back to you after our quick call a couple months ago. I can see you really need some guidance. I don't know how much time we'll have to chat at Kev's wedding tomorrow. How 'bout we get together for dinner on Sunday and really dig in on some of this?"

"Yeah, sure, that'd be great. How about a burger at Pete's around 5:00?"

"Sounds like a plan, man. See you tomorrow."

I breathe a sigh of relief. Okay. The cavalry is on the way. Maybe Vince can help me finally start to put some of this together in a cohesive manner.

Because business is bad. Really bad.

Last month another one of my people put in their notice. That makes three good employees gone in just a few months. And really, can I blame them? They're just not able to make a go of it. This last one hasn't even been with the agency that long and I had especially high hopes for him.

Lou was a natural – great personality, compassionate, hardworking, and really good with customers. I'd devoted a lot of time to training him, expecting that he would be a star.

But the poor guy just couldn't seem to get off the ground. There were simply no leads coming in that I could funnel his way, and the bottom line is that he's got a family to feed.

You'd think a guy in that situation wouldn't have such an aversion to cold calls, which is basically what it takes to get anywhere in this business. I mean, everybody hates making cold calls, but that's the only way to get clients and make money, right?

I fume and doodle on my legal pad.

And the customers – another few gone this week alone. At this point, Wakefield Insurance is pretty much *bleeding* money.

When will it end?

I log onto my computer for some research. I type 'car insurance' into the Google bar, and ads come up for three of the big national carriers, including the one that's the current thorn in my side – the clowns that just put up that stinking billboard down the street that I have to look at every. single. day.

Underneath those I see three local agents, with their addresses and even maps to their office locations.

Why the heck isn't my agency there? I know one of those agents is well over 70 years old and has probably never been on the internet in his life. And here I spend all day, every day on the internet and just put $6,000 into a new website!!

There are other agencies listed farther down, but none of them are local. And still, I don't see my website. What the heck is up with that?

You know, it seems like at least once a week I get an email from some random company claiming that my website isn't ranking for a bunch of different reasons that always look like gibberish to me. And claiming that they can put my website on Page 1.

Maybe I should think about contacting one of them. It's imperative that I get my website ranked decently so that I can get some traffic – and customers.

Looking back through some of the emails I've been sent by those companies, I select the one that doesn't seem to have any glaring spelling or grammatical errors. That alone makes them look a lot more legit than most of the others. They say they would be happy to provide a free website review to see if they can help.

Definitely something to think about.

One really cool thing about being in the insurance industry is that the product sold is not only something that everyone needs, but it's mandated by law. Therefore, your potential customer base is virtually anyone over the age of 15.

How can you let all of those consumers know about your business in a way that makes them want to choose *you* for their needs, rather than the agency down the street? How do you positively move potential customers to favor *you* over all the others?

Let's talk a little about branding. And by that, we don't mean what cowboys do to a cow's hind end.

Branding is a critical step in growing any business from a hand-to-mouth existence into true prosperity and self-sufficiency. Many people think that branding is just for large corporations, but as a small business owner, it's just as essential for you to have your own identifiable brand. And we're not talking about an insurance carrier's brand – we mean your own agency's distinctive brand.

Good, strong branding lets your customers and prospects know exactly who you are and what they can expect from you. So the first step is to sit down and determine what you stand for as a company.

What is the character of your business, your mission, your values? What do you want customers to think of when they hear your name? Jot down everything that pops into your mind.

Perhaps your list will include some of these:

- Honest
- High Integrity
- Compassionate
- Competent
- Professional
- Trustworthy
- Knowledgeable
- Caring
- Unique
- Likable
- Current
- Meticulous
- Friendly
- Expert
- Credible
- Exceptional

Now, being realistic, what do you think *actually* comes to people's minds when they hear your agency's name? What about when they see your logo or look at your website? Try to take a step back and be brutally honest.

Are you projecting a consistent image that aligns with your company's mission and values?

Unfortunately, most agencies tend to hang their shingle without paying proper attention whatsoever to developing a consistent brand.

This goes a long way toward explaining why so many small businesses fold after a short period of time. According to the Small Business Administration, fewer than 50% of new business start-ups make it to their 5th year.[3]

---

[3] Small Business Administration, Frequently Asked Questions about Small Business September 2012

At AMM, we begin with new clients by defining, creating and developing a world-class brand within the first 30 days, because in this competitive marketplace your agency simply *must* stand out. Clarity and consistency are vitally important in building your brand. Everything you or one of your employees does, says and writes contributes to your brand. As does personal appearance, the look of your offices, your logo, your website and on and on.

With a well managed, consistent brand, your customers and prospects, as well as potential employees and business partners, already know who you are and what you stand for. Simply from hearing your name, thoughts and memories will be evoked of your agency's personality and reputation, and folks will immediately know whether or not they want to be associated with you.

Good branding means that people will hardly need an introduction because they will feel that they know you. They'll already be warmed up, because your brand alone will have previously inspired their confidence.

Now let's talk about the importance of your website. Because your website is your online presence; your welcome mat, if you will. And more often than not, the outward perception when looking at an insurance agency's website is sloppy, ordinary, antiquated, uncaring and uninterested.

Let's face it, today most consumers begin any company interaction on the internet – like it or not. Recent data says that fully 74% of consumers research online before making a final decision.[4]

Would you like to write more commercial business and workplace benefits?

Businesses are *even more* likely than the average consumer to research potential agencies online. In fact, 94% of business buyers do some form of online research first.[5]

A few interesting things found among businesses researching online:

---

[4] J.D. Power 2016 U.S. Insurance Shopping Study
[5] A 2014 State of B2B Procurement study performed by Acquity Group

- 77% use Google search
- 84.3% check business websites
- 41% read user reviews

It's pretty clear that having a good, well thought-out website is absolutely critical. Is your website *all* that's important? Heck, no! But it's often the first introduction people have to your brand, and as such, it requires serious attention. So take a good, hard look at your website.

Your website should be:

- Welcoming
- Contemporary
- Relevant
- Clear
- Clean
- Easy-to-use
- Brand-consistent

You need to have multiple pages easily navigable by topic. Each page should have a specific purpose and be in keeping with your brand, from top to bottom, while prominently displaying your logo.

Content needs to include contemporary and relevant text, photos and graphics. If not, your prospects will presume that you're simply not up on all the latest and greatest in your industry. And if *you're* not, they'll continue their search elsewhere and you'll have lost them just that quickly.

An 'About Us' or 'Meet Our Team' page with photos and short bios on all of your employees is a *must*. It's that human connection that will give your visitors a feeling of comfort and familiarity – a feeling which may ultimately lead them to desire to do business with you, and which can even be beneficial in retaining existing customers.

Your website should primarily focus on how your agency is different from others; on exactly *why* someone should choose do business with you. If you don't currently have these differentiators, don't worry. You'll learn along with Jim how to create them in later chapters.

Provide *proof* of good service and show that you truly care about others in your community. Testimonials, photos and information about current and past events, accomplishments and community services should be highly visible.

Strive to add value to the experience your prospects and customers will have when they visit your website. Clean, simple websites tend to not only stand out, but also stand the test of time. Unless you want to be re-designing your website regularly, stay away from clutter and trends.

We've all heard the expression, *'You only get one chance to make a good first impression'*. Well, it's absolutely true. In this day and age of short attention spans, people tend to decide within a couple of seconds, or less, whether to take a further look at what you have to offer on your website. Do whatever you possibly can through the look, feel, branding and content to make sure your website has a fighting chance to retain their attention and goodwill.

Our friend Jim seems pretty excited about changing his logo and website.

Do you suppose that alone will solve all of his problems?

No way. But it's an important first step.

Let's check back in and see what he comes up with.

CHAPTER THREE
AND THE HITS JUST KEEP ON COMING

On Saturday afternoon, I watch my two ladies getting ready for The Big Wedding. Kevin, a life-long (we had thought) confirmed bachelor is finally tying the knot – to Cindy's best friend, Margie. With Margie's little boy from a previous marriage, they make a truly beautiful family.

They've sweetly made Kenzie a flower girl and she'll be walking down the aisle with Margie's son Eddie, who's the ring bearer. I'm going to be an usher and Cindy, the Matron of Honor.

I just love watching my girls together like this, Cindy looking radiant and giggling with Ken. It's wonderful to see her so happy and excited for once.

I've got to be the luckiest guy in the world to have these two in my life. But I'm desperately afraid I'm going to let my wife down, and Kenzie too, if I can't figure out all my stuff at work and get the agency turned around.

It turns out to be an unusually beautiful, touching wedding. Big, strong ex-football player Kevin has tears running down his face as they say their 'I Do's'. Cindy openly sobs, and I have to confess, I get pretty choked up, too. Ain't love grand?

As the ceremony concludes, a new family now, Margie and Kevin put Eddie between them and all swing hands, laughing as they walk back down the aisle.

Later on, I scan the ballroom as Cindy and I chat with Margie and Kevin, all four of us watching the two best friends, Kenzie and

Eddie, race around the room together, enjoying the celebration. The kids are both so charged up already, I can't imagine what they're going to be like once they get some sugary wedding cake in them!

I finally spy Vince at the bar and quickly excuse myself. Coming up behind him, I say, "Hey, man, can I buy you a beer?"

We greet each other warmly, shaking hands while giving the one-armed-hug/manly-back-thump characteristic of the male of our species. Then we stroll onto the covered terrace, where we sit chatting with our beers for a few minutes, just catching up with each other.

"Tell me, Vince, what is it about free beer that makes it taste so much better than the swill you have to pay for?"

"Ah, truly a question for the ages, Jimbo. I always said you were a deep thinker."

"Hey, it's a burden to be this bright and insightful, let me tell you. But we all have our crosses to bear."

"That we do, my friend. That we do. Hey, do we have to keep pretending that we're manly enough to tough it out in subzero temperatures, or can we go back in now? February weddings are beautiful, but it's pretty nippy when the sun goes down."

"I think our manly status is secure. Let's go see if Eddie and Kenzie have any new moves on the dance floor. Watching them is a hoot! Eddie is such a funny kid. He always cracks me up."

As we rejoin our friends and family I can't help but wish things could always be this happy. Because I know that as soon as we get home, Cindy and I will be right back to treating each other like strangers. If I can't get things hammered out with the agency soon, I'm afraid the pressure is going to kill our family.

The next evening, I drive to an early dinner with Vince after spending the whole of Sunday at the office. I'm reflecting over the complete mess my life seems to be right now. Things have been going from bad to worse with Cindy. We're not talking – or doing much of anything else – lately.

Her frosty silence is really beginning to get to me and my stress is spiraling out of control. I've even started getting chest pains, which I'm trying hard to ignore.

A block before Pete's, I spy a huge billboard and groan. Really, guys? I so didn't need to see that right now. That same freakin' thorn from Google the other morning. They've decided they want to be #1 in the state for auto insurance, and they're *everywhere* right now – billboards, TV, online, newspaper ads, snail mail – telling all of my clients and potential clients that they're idiotically throwing money away if they don't switch.

Why the heck did they have to pick *my* state? Aren't things bad enough right now?

Because honestly, if people can save some money, why wouldn't they switch? Times are tough. But it sure feels personal. And it's getting harder and harder to roll with the punches when it's affecting every aspect of my life – my business, my finances, my health, my happiness, even my relationship with my wife.

Pretty discouraging.

I finally pull into the parking lot at Pete's a little before 5:00 and grab a booth near the back. As I wait for Vince, I get out my notebook hoping I'll get some good stuff from him that I can put to use right away.

I see Vince walk in the front door and wave him over.

"Hey, man, how's it goin'?"

"It pretty much sucks, Vince. How's it going for you?"

"Excellent, dude! And listen, we're gonna get you some help tonight, I promise. So let's order. I'm starving!"

The waitress deposits a frosty pitcher of beer on our table tells us our burgers will be up soon. After taking a couple of long, refreshing gulps, I sit back and feel calmer for the first time during this very long and stressful day. I close my eyes for a moment and breathe a sigh of relief, feeling my blood pressure start to level out.

"OK, Jim, now that you're appreciating the simple pleasures in life – cause, man it just doesn't get much better than a cold beer and a hot burger – let's talk about your problems. How'd your logo and website come out?"

"Here, I brought my laptop. You tell me."

Vince sips his beer as he scrolls through the pages on the agency's site.

"Well, I gotta say, this is a whole lot better. I like the logo. It's cool, fresh, contemporary. Nice job. And the website is much cleaner and easier to use. I think that basically, your designers did a pretty good job. Congrats, man."

"Well, that's a relief. Because let me tell you, it was expensive, and I'm getting dangerously close to being tapped out here. I *have* to get some new customers, Vince. *Fast*. And figure out how to hold on to the ones I already have. I lost three more just this week!"

"Sounds like before we talk about anything else, we should really work on how you can do a better job of retaining your customers. Because getting new customers is immaterial if you can't hold on to them – you're just like a hamster on a wheel, running, running, running and never getting anywhere. *Huge* waste of time and energy – not to mention money – am I right?"

"Tell me about it."

"So, what exactly do you do to hold on to them?"

"Umm. Not sure what you mean. I think we give great customer service. Solid, friendly, reliable. I make sure of it."

"Yeeeaahh. But so do a lot of other agencies. Is your service better than the agency down the street? Than the one over on the next block? How 'bout the place I can see across the street from us right now or that big ol' billboard I saw on my way over? Do you think they probably give decent service, too?"

"OK, I get your point. We're probably all about the same. I'm selling insurance, they're selling insurance. It's a commodity. Hopefully, my rates are sometimes lower; hopefully, my customers are lazy and aren't surfing the internet looking for lower prices. What do you want from me?"

"Tell me what you're doing, specifically, to give them a reason to stay with *you*."

"I'm really not getting what you're saying," as I'm beginning to get a little annoyed now.

Vince asks, "How do you show them that you care?"

"I don't know, man. But I do, *genuinely*, care about them and their families, about their futures."

"Hey, I know you do, Jim. But where's the proof? If I'm your customer, how do I *know* you care about me?"

I burst out, "Because I provide you with value! I protect you and your family! I ensure that you'll have the ability to get through the absolute worst life has to throw at you with as little pain and struggle as possible!"

"You *sure* that's true?"

"I *know* it's true! I see what's happening to families out there every day! I talk to so many people, all the time, who are making *huge* mistakes! Folks who don't have the proper coverage on their car, who are literally flushing their money down the drain because they're doing nothing more than making sure they don't break the law by driving without insurance!

"Homeowners who have no idea what is and isn't covered in their policies, and then make bad decisions about when to file and not file a claim."

I continue, speaking faster and faster, as all the frustrations of the past weeks come tumbling out.

"Unbelievable as it seems, lots of families out there don't even have a *nominal* life insurance policy to help them get through what will be the most horrible time of their lives, without losing their home and uprooting them from everything they know and care about!

"Man, I talk to people every single day who, for all practical purposes, are stashing their money *under their mattresses* because they don't know there are financial products available that would allow them to protect themselves and their families and take advantage of rising markets with no risk!"

I'm pretty fired-up, now. "Regardless of what you might think, Vince, I *know* what I'm doing and I care *deeply* about my customers. What the hell more can I do?"

Vince speaks quietly. "You can *show* them that you care. *I* know that you care about all those people, Jim, because I know you, and we've built a solid relationship over time."

He continues, "Listen, what I'm getting at here is that you need to keep your customers engaged. You can't just touch base once a year at renewal time and think that's all that needs to happen in order to get their undying loyalty."

I sigh, feeling spent after my rant. "Well, we email birthday cards to them, too."

"OK. That's good. So that's twice a year you contact them. What of value are you bringing them the other 10 months out of the year?"

I say nothing.

"You don't do a newsletter?"

"No. Saying what? 'Gimme more business, please?' That's lame."

"Well, sure, if that's all the newsletter does, it's lame. But I'm talking about reaching out and touching these guys with something of real value once a month. Something that will bring your agency to mind in a positive way, repeatedly, throughout the year. Something that lets your customers know that you care about them and are a real part of their lives. Something that will *build relationships*."

I sigh again and slump back in the booth.

"OK, let's try this: when customers and prospects come into your office, how much of the conversation is about the insurance stuff – policies, rates and coverages?"

"Probably about 10, maybe 20%," I quickly calculate.

"And what about the rest of the time?"

"The rest of the time is just shooting the breeze – getting to know them a little bit. Finding out about them and their families, and what's important to them. You know. Bonding."

Jumping up, Vince yells, "EXACTLY!", and gives a few slow claps. Astonished for a moment, I just stare at him. Then I finally crack a smile and motion him to sit down.

"Go on," I say, knowing that Vince may actually get to his point now.

"BOOM! You *finally* hit the nail on the head, my friend! You shoot the breeze and try to get to know them, find out what's important to them and *bond*," Vince says excitedly. "That's big-time, important stuff, right?"

He continues, "But dude, it shouldn't end there – it needs to go on for the *lifetime* of each customer. And since you can't possibly have those conversations with thousands of people every single month, you have to find an alternate way to communicate with them.

"So lemme ask you this: do you know the difference between *Contacts* and *Contracts*?"

I'm baffled and think about it for a few moments. So that Vince won't think I'm an idiot, I spit out a vague definition of each.

Vince replies, "Nope. *Contracts* has an 'r' in the middle."

I give Vince my *'Are you kidding me?'* stoney gaze.

"OK, sorry. Here you go – it's all about the 'r', baby. *Relationships*."

"And?"

"Think of it like this. You have this contact. You know his name is Joe Blow, his phone number is 555-444-3333 and his email address is joe@whogivesashit.com. You don't know anything about him, and he doesn't know anything about you except that you sold him some insurance.

"That's a contact," Vince says.

He continues, "But if you really *know* him, Jimbo, you know that Joe is married to Susan and they have 2 beautiful kids and a Labrador retriever, and that they love to go out on their boat as a family every weekend.

"If you really care about him, you've reached out and touched him throughout the year. You've provided value to his family's lives, so that they know you, like you, and *trust* you. They've come to know what you stand for, and that you're always helping the folks around you to live well and thrive."

Vince is the one on a roll now.

"That's the magical 'r', my friend. That's a *relationship*. Joe is not going to leave you for the flavor-of-the-month, or because some jackass puts 9000 billboards up all around town or because some other guy can save him $5 or $10 a month. Joe's in it for the long haul because he truly thinks of you as his trusted advisor.

"Answer me this – what's the average customer retention for an insurance agency?"

I actually know this, because I'd been looking into it when it seemed like too many customers were bailing. "About 84 - 90%".

Vince nods his head, "Great. Let's say it's 87% then. So what's the retention in your agency?"

I knew it was coming so immediately say, "Only about 82%."

Then strangely, Vince smiles and exclaims, "Awesome! I smell opportunity, my man!"

I raise an eyebrow. "Do tell."

"Did you know that a 5% increase in retention leads to a 25% - 85% increase in profitability, depending on the business type?"

Vince is getting excited again and begins talking quickly. "And if I remember correctly, in the insurance business they calculate it to be a 50% increase in profitability. It's based on a lot of factors, including an increase in policies purchased, increase in referrals and reduction in operating costs. But anyway, the point is that you just need to get up to that average of 87%. *Then* you can strive for another 50% profitability increase and go for 92%!"

"When you put it like that, it sounds pretty damn good!" I nod, grinning now. Of course, I love the idea of a 50% increase in profit. Who wouldn't? I really hadn't realized the enormous effect retention could have on my business.

"OK… you think I should start with a newsletter. But how do I go about it? It sounds expensive."

"Doesn't necessarily have to be. But you have to know your numbers, Jim, and the return on investment. Figure out how much a monthly publication would cost you vs. your potential profit. Do you know how much your average customer is worth over the time they're with you?"

I shake my head.

"What about how much it currently costs you to acquire a new customer?"

I squirm. "Not so much."

Vince gets more serious. "You *gotta* know your numbers, man. How else are you gonna know how much you can spend?"

"Point taken. I'll get right on it. Meanwhile, I'm sold on the newsletter idea. Sooo," I pause and shrug. "What do I even put in it?"

"Do the numbers first. And then…you're a bright guy, Jim. I bet you can figure it out. Put yourself in your customers' shoes. What would *you* like to see in a newsletter that hits your inbox once a month? Just keep in mind what a wise man once said was the #1 rule of marketing - *Don't be boring.*"

As I drive home from my dinner with Vince, I feel a little more optimistic. At least now I have a plan of action and can see how essential it is to plug my retention gap before my business is completely drained.

Back at the office on Monday morning, I get my coffee and deliberately don't look at my email. I can't let my plans for the day get derailed by fire-fighting, at least not for the next couple of hours.

I take a deep breath and sit down. Sadly, even though I love math, Vince made me realize that I'm really not on top of the numbers for my own business like I should be. Kind of reckless, considering I'm risking my family's entire future on this agency, not to mention the futures of my employees and their families, too.

Time to change all that.

I open up my legal pad and review the notes from our dinner yesterday. Vince pointed out the stats I need to know, and also how to best calculate them.

I list each on the whiteboard in my office and then bring up my customer management application to run a report showing how many customers I had at the beginning of the prior year. Then I move back over to jot the figure down on my whiteboard.

I quickly calculate how much money I gave up last year by not having the average 87% rate of retention, instead of my current 82% retention.

$16,000. I underline it, scowling.

Boy oh boy, I sure could have used that extra $1,500 a month in my bank account!

Cindy and I could've taken a nice summer vacation out west like we always talk about, so that I could show my girls some of the amazing sights I remember from my family travels as a kid.

Not only that, the credit cards would be all paid off by now, and there would still have been enough left over to invest back into the agency, instead of everything being so damn tight.

Oh, well; it's water under the bridge and there's no use crying over spilled milk. I shake my head.

Continuing my calculations, I find that my average yearly customer revenue is $248.

The agency's previous owner had told me that a customer was worth about $100 a year, but his reasoning had been faulty. He had been thinking of just one auto policy, and the majority of customers actually have multiple policies.

Of course, I have customers who only have renters insurance, which brings in about $15/year...but I'll stick with my calculations as an average customer revenue of $248 per year. That's a no-brainer – numbers don't lie and an average is an average.

Using my sorry 82% retention, I then figure up each customer's lifetime value. It comes in at $1,378.

Wow. I ponder that for a minute. That seems pretty good, even given my low retention.

I soon realize that while I have no problem performing the calculations, there are some things I'm not sure exactly *how* to accurately measure. Such as how much it costs me to acquire a new customer. With no consistent acquisition process, how can I accurately determine that cost?

The only source of acquiring customers I really have experience with is buying internet leads, which I stopped doing because we were closing only 2% of them. But let me go ahead and see what the numbers are for those.

Moving to my desk a moment later, I sit staring at the number on the whiteboard in front of me.

Each new customer I got from a purchased internet lead was costing me *$1,000*.

And since my customers are only earning me $1,378 over their entire lifetime, those leads were practically putting me in a hole after paying my team.

Whew, I'm so glad I stopped buying those leads when I did!

I sit in my chair and stare at the numbers on the whiteboard. My eyes and attention gravitate back to retention.

And then it hits me…

I feel sick to my stomach as I methodically perform the calculations and add the results to my board. Unless I improve retention, I will be missing out on over **$560,000 of profit**.

That's only considering my *current customers* and the difference between an 82% retention and 87% retention over the customer lifetime. Whoa.

I mutter to myself, "Retention… retention… retention."

The nearby desk phone rings, startling me out of my current bewilderment. Paul, one of my remaining sales producers has a question from a prospective customer that he can't seem to answer.

Derailed from my mission once again, I realize my investigation into a newsletter will have to wait. But, hey, at least I was able to get my numbers together before the usual Monday Madness took over.

AGENCY #'S

RETENTION

82% WANT 87%

AVG CUSTOMER LIFETIME

5.6 YrS WANT 7.7 Yrs

AVG CUSTOMER LIFETIME VALUE

$1,378 WANT $1,908

GAP: $530
X 1,058 CUSTOMERS

= $560,650 LOST PROFIT

Vince's text message at the beginning of the chapter is absolutely right. Looking at your website as the end-all-be-all of your marketing will get you nowhere fast. By referencing *'Field of Dreams'*, he meant that businesses often think all they need to do is get a website up and prospects will come beating down the door. But, "If you build it, they will come," simply isn't the case. At all.

Vince certainly didn't mean to get Jim off on the wrong foot when he commented on the Wakefield website during their initial phone call, but it was the first thing he saw and the only information he had on Jim's agency. And, of course, the reality is that your website is often the first thing your prospects see, as well.

Now, we've reviewed a whole lot of insurance agency websites and have to say that the typical agency site is just not good. Not good at all.

Therefore, having a well-designed, clean and contemporary website is a great start. But it's just a start. There is *so much more* that goes into having a website which will enhance the customer experience and generate business for you. We'll be expanding on those concepts little by little throughout the remainder of our time together in this book.

Right now, let's see what we can do to improve customer retention so that as your marketing efforts begin to bear the fruit of more and more customers, you'll have a better chance of hanging on to them.

Because building relationships takes time and patience.

However, it truly *is* the only way to realize significant and lasting success in a service-oriented industry. Why? Because in order to build a thriving insurance agency, and in order to make money, you have to build a client base that trusts you and is loyal to you over the long haul.

And what's the best way to do that? Through the building of relationships.

Put yourself in your customers' shoes. They write a check once a month (or once a year) for something they can't really *see*; something they can't really *touch*. Insurance is a nebulous commodity. They can't play with it, admire it in their homes or really *enjoy* it in any way, other than the peace of mind it brings.

Now, granted, peace of mind is huge. But they can get the same peace of mind from using the agency down the street or some guy on the internet – it doesn't have to come from you.

So exactly how do we as human beings build relationships?

We build relationships by showing people that we care about them.

Think of your significant other. Did he or she love and trust you overnight? Probably not. You had to slowly show them that you cared about them and that you could be trusted. Over time, you worked yourselves into each other's lives in an enduring way. It's the same way with friendships. Lasting relationships of any kind are gradually built over time, as you get to know each other and trust is deepened.

Why would business be any different? After all, you're asking people to trust you and stay with you for years…for decades…for their entire lives. And hopefully, to recommend their friends to you.

The study[6] that Vince referenced was initially published in the Harvard Business Review back in 1990 and has held up in the years since, proving to be extremely influential in the business

---

[6] Zero Defections: Quality Comes to Services, by Frederick F. Reichheld and W. Earl Sasser, Jr., Frederick F. Reichheld, W. Earl Sasser, Jr. September-October 190 Harvard Business Review

world. A 50% increase in profitability with a 5% increase in customer retention certainly gets our attention – how about *you?*

I mean, we *want* customers to stick around, don't we? One of the main reasons insurance is such an attractive career is due to the residual income. Year after year we reap the rewards of retaining our customers' business. So, yeah, we want to hang on to every single customer for as long as we possibly can.

In fact, it's *so* important, that it would behoove us to focus a whole lot of our time and energy on it, don't you think?

Another thing Vince discussed with Jim was the necessity of knowing his numbers. One of the big reasons many small businesses struggle and fail is because they don't bother to stay on top of the critical numbers which drive their business.

*Download a copy of the same essential numbers and calculations to use for your own agency at www.AgentsOfChangebook.com/resources.

Jim's newsletter will be a terrific first step toward getting personal and building lasting relationships that will increase customer retention. Because a quality publication that is seen by customers and prospects each and every month keeps the agency front and center in their minds, giving real value to your brand and increasing retention and referrals.

Jim is at a crucial point in the life of his agency and in his attempt to institute marketing that will bring in more clients... clients who will stay with him for the duration. We see these challenges affecting virtually every aspect of his life, because our professional and personal lives are so deeply intertwined, aren't they?

It's time to check back in with Jim to see if he's able to effect positive change before he and his agency crumble altogether.

CHAPTER FOUR
WE REACH CRITICAL MASS

Driving to the office a couple of weeks later, I notice flower bulbs just beginning to poke their heads up along the side of the road. Spring is on the way, but I've barely noticed. All of my energy has been focused on researching whether or not producing a good quality newsletter will help to develop the relationships necessary to hang on to more of my customers.

From what I've learned, I'm impressed with Vince's first bit of concrete advice. It turns out that not only are newsletters hugely effective, they're one of the top three tools used by business-to-business marketers today. Some solid commercial clients surely would help my current situation.

But these publications seem to be equally effective with the average Joe, because they promote exactly what Vince said they did – a personal connection that, over time, builds a trusting relationship.

Unfortunately, my research also suggests that a newsletter is something I may not see any real results from for at least six months. It would have been great if I could have counted on a more immediate return – shoot, at this point, I don't even know if I'll still be in business in six months – but I have to try.

The harsh reality is that I just don't know how much longer I'm going to be able to keep the agency's doors open if things don't start to turn around significantly.

Even if I ultimately need to sell the business, I've got to believe that having this in the pipeline will make my agency more attractive, and perhaps even a better investment, to a potential buyer. How depressing. The thought of selling makes me sick to my stomach. But most days I feel like I'm paddling furiously simply to keep my head above water. And I'm afraid that I'm slowly losing the battle.

So if a newsletter has even the *possibility* of helping to build relationships with customers and prospects, relationships which will develop trust in me and my staff so that customers will stay longer and maybe even bundle more policies, the bottom line is that I need to get this started *now*.

When I arrive at the office, first in, as has been the case the past few months, I see an email from the SEO company I've been in contact with. They told me they could eventually get the Wakefield website to Page 1 for the bargain price of $500 a month.

It drives me crazy to think of my beautiful new website just sitting there collecting digital dust when I spent so much time and money on it. But I know that relationship-building takes time and I need to do *something* to get the phone to ring right now. I simply can't keep wrestling with the same old problems day after day. And maybe this will help.

Sighing, I sign the electronic contract and enter my agency AmEx to pay for the first month's fee.

Afterwards, I try to get back to work, but am unable to concentrate on anything else. Something just doesn't feel right.

$500 a month is a *lot* of money. And although I'm good at math and science, I really don't understand web technology or search engine marketing at all. Why the heck didn't I get Vince's opinion before committing to this SEO company? I guess maybe I wanted him to think I could handle some of this marketing stuff on my own, and impress him once I was King of Google.

Well, better late than never. I bite the bullet and pick up my phone.

Amazingly enough, Vince answers the phone without it going to voicemail. That's gotta be a first. I quickly explain the current situation and wait for his reaction with bated breath.

Vince is silent for a moment, then says, "OK. Let me see if I have this straight. These guys say if you give them $500 every month, through search engine optimization they'll get you to Page 1 for searches in your city of auto and homeowners insurance? I hate to break the bad news to you, Jim, but I seriously doubt it.

"These companies are the scourge of the entire marketing industry, man! They send *hundreds of thousands* of emails to businesses, knowing that a whole lot of people will bite simply because they don't know any better. Hell, SEO companies have pilfered more money from hard-working small businesses than the mafia! They just don't use a baseball bat to do it. Well, at least, not that I know of, anyway," Vince chuckles.

"Great."

"Did they guarantee your Page 1 placement within a certain period of time or your money back? No, don't bother to answer, because I already know the answer. Did they at least detail exactly what they would be doing every month in order to accomplish this feat?"

"No, there's nothing spelled out in the agreement," I sigh.

Vince responds, "Hmm. So let's say you somehow, miraculously, picked the *one* legitimate SEO company out there, and they manage to get you to third place on the maps listing. What exactly is the return on investment you were expecting to see from that $500 a month?"

"I honestly don't know. But it seems like people search online for everything these days, so it must be important to be listed where they can actually find me."

"Well, Jim, let's think this through together.

"How many of the people who saw your listing on Page 1, and in the top 3 of the local business listings with maps, would you expect to click through and access your website to fill out your 'get a quote' form? Or call you?

"And would you expect them to be decent leads? Or absolute crap that wouldn't close at any kind of a worthwhile rate and wouldn't stick with you for any length of time, just like those internet leads you used to buy? See, it all relates back to what we've been talking about for the last couple of months.

Vince speaks softly, with genuine concern in his voice. "I don't mean to badger you about this, buddy, but I just don't want to see you waste any more of your precious time and money. And, trust me, you're not alone. This is such a common trap that I see businesses fall into time and time again with their marketing budgets."

I don't respond. I'm too busy kicking myself for not investigating this more thoroughly before spending money that I really don't have in the first place.

Vince continues, "Listen, I know you're a numbers analyst at heart, and that's good. Because this is an area where we can at least make some educated guesses. I've seen companies dump *hundreds of thousands of dollars* on SEO, and then Google, bless its little heart, ups and changes the ranking algorithms or number of listings to display, and – POOF! – they're no longer ranking. It's a bitter lesson to learn first-hand, I kid you not.

"So, Jim, the bottom line is, do you want to invest considerable funds in something that seems like a quick fix, but could be gone in a moment? Or do you want to work toward marketing activities that are *reliable* and *replicable*? Activities especially crafted to provide long-term success not tied to the whims of some other company that doesn't care about your agency at all?"

"Yeah. I get what you're saying, Vince. I should've known it was too good to be true. I feel sick that I already gave them $500."

"Well hey, man, live and learn, right? Try not to beat yourself up about it too much. Anyway, fire those clowns immediately and change any permissions or passwords you gave them. If they won't give you a refund, just chalk it up to a lesson learned. At least you learned it before you'd given them any *more* money, and before they messed you up so that you were actually in an even *worse* position in the rankings. 'Cause I've seen it happen.

"Just please, please, concentrate your efforts on what we discussed – namely, ways to build relationships. Because *that* is the real deal, man."

I nod, agreeing.

Vince added, "I'll email you a few inexpensive resources you can utilize on your own for SEO. Sorry, I should've thought to get them to you earlier, but I've just been swamped."

Later in the day I look down at the notepad in front of me. Vince gave me some basic guidelines of internal research that will allow me to evaluate the viability of a newsletter for the agency.

After doing some digging, the results are quite interesting:
- Total customers: 1,058
- Customers with emails: 741
- Total contacts, including non-customers: 3,440
- Total contacts with addresses: 1,588
- Total contacts with emails: 1,675

I'm surprised by how many people are actually in my system especially considering how bad I am myself about logging each prospect into the CRM program. It's really too bad the previous owner hadn't bothered to capture email addresses, but I've had my staff calling every customer so that we can add it to their contact record.

I'm sure we haven't sent emails to even half of these folks. Still, I feel torn because I really hate to bother people – I don't want them to think that I'm just trying to sell them something and get them to part with more of their hard-earned money.

Anyway, I always kind of figured most people were bored by insurance. They don't *really* want to hear from me, do they? It always seems so much like a one-way street in an email, with me asking for something and providing them with nothing in return.

But with Vince's quality newsletter idea, I guess it turns those notions upside down. Maybe I can reverse that one-way street and give these 1,675 folks something of value. That could be exciting. That could change things.

Maybe it's just a matter of mindset – that instead of always asking for something, I'm providing something of value – something enjoyable – something that will even educate at times. Perhaps my customers will finally see me as an important part of their lives. And maybe over time they'll even begin to see just how important this relationship truly could be in achieving their goals.

Looking at my whiteboard with the calculations on my Customer Lifetime Value, I'm still a little shocked to see the difference between my current retention of 82% and my current goal of 87%.

$530.

I can make an extra $530 per customer by getting my retention to 87%.

Vince says that my first step towards that goal is to look into publishing a monthly newsletter for my customers to strengthen those relationships.

And just what *is* the investment needed to do that? Well, I'm not exactly sure yet. But roughly estimating – maybe $1 per newsletter per month in printing and postage.

So… at 87% my average customer lifetime would be 7.7 years. And at $1 per month my total investment there would be about $92.

$92 investment per customer to get me $530? I like the look of that.

OK, so that's my current customers. But what about converting a prospect into a customer? I move over to the whiteboard.

$12 newsletter cost per year / $248 commission per customer per year = 4.8%

So, just to break even on turning a prospect into a customer in one year of mailing, I need to have a 4.8% conversion rate… roughly 1 new customer for every 20 prospects who receive the newsletter over the course of a year.

I've already done the research on direct mail campaigns and found that 1 - 2% is achievable for single mailings. So with 12 mailings needing a 5% conversion rate seems possible.

Especially considering that the lifetime value of that new customer would be $1,378-$1,908, depending on my retention, not just $248.

Yes, I would be willing to spend $248 to get back maybe $1,900! That's pretty much a no-brainer.

The numbers seem to work if the newsletter will help my retention at all, and also bring in more customers. Not only that, it should help me sell more to existing customers.

I hear the front door open and remember that I have a meeting with a client to review their insurance policies, to be followed up with a conference call, and then another meeting to finish off the day. Time to put my project back on hold.

The next day, I take another look at the whiteboard and shake my head. The printer has sent a final quote. For a four-page newsletter in black and white, mailed to my database, it will cost $1,461 per month.

Even though this is less than the $1 per newsletter that I was estimating yesterday, seeing the full monthly cost is fairly scary.

I have a good relationship with my printer, so am pretty confident I've gotten the best deal possible on bulk printing and postage, folding, and the stickers needed to hold the piece together.

Since my research found that I shouldn't expect to see any real results for at least 6 months, I'm looking at a spending at least $8,766 before seeing even one single dollar back.

Jeez…am I going to have to get a loan just to invest in my marketing?!

Man, oh, man. I can't swallow the idea of incurring more debt.

And, of course, I still have to come up with the content – compelling articles, good images and photos. It's more than a little overwhelming. I feel a tightness in my chest and take a deep breath. *Think,* Jim! There *has* to be a way through this.

Since Vince has impressed upon me the value of printed newsletters as the best way to go, I pick up the phone and fill him in on my findings of the last couple days.

Vince whistles. "Yeah, I can understand your hesitation, man. That's a large number of contacts - more than I had thought, actually. Given that, it might not be the right timing for you, cash flow-wise, to make that investment. No worries. Instead, concentrate on getting it off the ground by distributing via email."

"Yeah, but then I seem just like every other guy out there who sends out a dumb email newsletter for awhile, then realizes it's lame, and stops," I quickly respond back.

Vince starts to get excited, "No, you won't be like everyone else. Because you're smarter than that, dude. You're going to shake things up. Include the cool things those other boring newsletters don't have."

"I was really hoping to send printed newsletters," I sighed.

Vince added, "It's true that print copies are ideal, because then you can give it to folks when they come into the office and it becomes a sales piece to walk through all the stuff that makes your agency different. People can take it home and show it to their spouses. They can see printed proof of why it's worth switching agencies, and it also reinforces their decision to place their business with you. Without a doubt, that's all great. But the most important thing here is to get going *now* with something you can afford. So...let me think a minute..." Vince pauses for several seconds before resuming.

"OK, here's an idea to get maximum value out of your email campaign: create an *awesome community magazine*! Instead of black and white, make it vibrant; eye-catching; fun. Link it to all the places on your website that customers and prospects need to visit to see how great you guys are. But in order to reflect highly on your agency, it has to actually *be* of high quality – no templated Word doc with images copied out of Google searches."

I quickly jot down these points.

"I'll send you over the names of a couple graphic designers I've worked with who're always looking for side jobs and are reasonably priced. Since you're gonna be able to send this out for next to nothing, you need to invest a little more in the design and totally blow this baby out, Jim!"

"That sounds great, Vince, thanks. I really appreciate your help!"

Several days later, on a Friday evening, I sit at my desk with my head in my hands. Mindy's been out since the previous Friday recuperating from minor surgery, and things are chaotic. I've spent the entire week doing her job as well as my own, while trying to get a handle on my marketing/research/customer/employee woes.

To top it all off, Paul called in sick again today, because his ulcer is acting up. Gotta feel kind of responsible for that. Because business is getting progressively worse.

Eventually, I drag myself out the door a little after 7:00 p.m., a situation which is becoming all-too-normal for me.

What really concerns me on my drive home is the nagging feeling that I forgot something important. Jimbo, you've got to make sure to look at your calendar and To-Do List even when you're slammed, buddy. Oh, well, I'll go in tomorrow and put out whatever additional fire I've unwittingly created for himself.

I park in the garage and enter the house through the kitchen around 7:30. Everything seems kind of dark and quiet; that's odd. I peek into the living room. Just one soft light on. As I walk through the room, something catches my eye in the dining room. I pause in the doorway, taking in the scene. In the mirror on the opposite wall, I see horror etched on my face.

Candlelight, linens, china, wine glasses – and I finally realize what it is that's been lurking at the back of my mind all day.

Our 15th wedding anniversary.

Holy crap.

I promised Cindy I'd be home early to celebrate. Racing up the stairs, I find my wife sitting on the edge of the bed in tears.

"Honey, I'm *so* sorry. I'm a complete and total ass."

As Cindy replies, "Yes. You are," I kneel and put my arms around her.

"Why, Jim? I was going to remind you this morning, but you left so early that I didn't have a chance to. *And I shouldn't have to!*"

"Cindy, you're absolutely right. There's no excuse. I got slammed at work. Mindy's still out from her surgery, Paul called in sick, and it flew right out of my mind. I'm so, so sorry, honey. I *promise* I'll make it up to you."

"When? Because Jim, it's not just tonight. It's every night! I'm clearly just not important to you anymore," she sobs.

"Cindy, you *are*. You and Kenzie are the *most* important things in my life. But..."

"But what?!"

"But I've been having some...unusually tough situations at work to deal with lately."

"What, Jim? What could possibly be more important than our 15th anniversary?"

I sit on the floor, running my hands through my hair. Maybe it's time to finally tell Cindy the truth. After a minute I say, "Babe, why don't we go downstairs and get a glass of wine. I guess I have some stuff I need to tell you."

Over an hour later, Cindy and I are still at the dining room table, the remains of our reheated dinner before us. Cindy gets up and pours us both another glass of wine, saying, "At least Kenzie's at my mom's for the night. Honey, you should have told me what you've been going through. This is a *partnership*, isn't it? We share the bad times, not just the good ones – it was in our vows, remember? That's what marriage *is*."

"I know. And I'm sorry. But I was just trying to protect you."

"How does that protect me? Here I've been thinking all *kinds* of crazy things, alternately feeling furious, terrified and sorry for myself, at a time when you needed my support and understanding the most." She sighs. "Well, at least I know now. And you're not in this alone. Shame on you for thinking that you were!"

"I know, babe. I'm an idiot."

"You are, but you're my idiot," she says as she leans over to kiss my cheek. She turns serious again. "Do you want to try to sell out, Jim? Go back to teaching?"

I think for a few moments and then shake my head. "I don't think so. Even if I *could* find a buyer…even if we *wouldn't* lose our shirts in the deal…I don't know. It just doesn't feel right."

"Tell me this…Why did you want to buy this insurance agency in the first place?"

"I liked the idea of being my own boss. Of *helping* people. Customers *and* employees. Insurance seemed like a good fit for those reasons, but also because I saw the income potential. The residual income that can build over time is just phenomenal, Cin. And *everyone* out there has to have what we sell – by law!

"But you know, what I loved most about teaching was the interaction with the kids, helping them, guiding them, being a trusted advisor to them. I really thought I could do that on a larger scale for my clients and their families. Improve their lives. Improve this *community* that we love. Build a better world for Kenzie. Does that sound crazy?"

"No, sweetheart, it sounds like the wonderful man I married. You'll find a way of out this, Jim, I'm *sure* of it. And I agree. I think sticking with the business is the best thing for you, and for our family, and we'll find a way to make it work. *Together*. I know we will. Come on, it's getting late. Let's go to bed and celebrate 15 years together."

"You're on!"

Driving to work on Monday morning, I'm feeling more positive for the first time in a very long time. Just getting it all out in the open with Cindy has been a huge relief. It's true – a problem shared really is a problem halved, and she couldn't have been more helpful and supportive.

We spent the whole weekend hashing some things out together, and we finally seem like a team again. I had forgotten just how great that could feel. An idea occurs to me, and I swing by Krispy Kreme to pick up a dozen donuts and a big carafe of coffee.

I catch myself whistling as I walk in the agency door, and smile. Cindy has reminded me of one very important thing – I'm not in this alone. I have a built-in support system; I just have to figure out how to best utilize it. And for the first time in forever, I feel a glimmer of hope for the future.

Putting the donuts and coffee on the conference room table, I rally the troops.

"Hey, Boss, what gives? You welcoming me back?"

I used to cringe when Mindy called me 'Boss', but I got used to it and now it cracks me up.

"I am, actually, welcoming you back, Mindy. It's great to see your smiling face. We missed you, didn't we guys? But it's more than that – I'm welcoming us all to a new day...a new team...a new agency."

Paul pipes up, "Whoa! Are you trying to tell us you're selling out, Jim? Because I knew things weren't great, I think we all did. But is it really time to throw in the towel?"

"Not even close, guys! Don't get nervous! It's just that, yeah, things haven't been good. And I don't think I've been going about this the right way. I thought I was shouldering that knowledge alone, but apparently, you guys have been picking up on it anyway.

I go on, "I know you've seen it in your paychecks, and I also know that I haven't been much fun to be around, lately."

"You're telling us! No, just kidding," jokes Melissa, who is my other remaining sales producer, along with Paul.

Mindy pipes up, "Well, you have been riding us pretty hard lately, it's true. But we love you even when you're a jerk."

"Well, hey, at least you guys can joke about it. But I apologize. Truly. And ladies and gentlemen, I've had an epiphany."

"Ouch. Was it painful?" Beth is my other customer service rep and was with the prior owner for 20 years before I bought the agency. She's sort of a mother hen, and always likes to keep the mood light with bad jokes.

"Always the comedian, Beth. Yeah, actually it was. But only because it was such a long time in coming. My wife reminded me of something very important this weekend – I'm not in this alone. We're a *team*, all of us, and we're going to start acting like it.

"Wakefield Insurance is going to start focusing on *building relationships* like never before. Building relationships with our customers and prospects, and building relationships with each other, too. I have it on good authority that this is what will propel our agency forward. Not just in the short-term, but over the long haul, generating business month after month, year after year and decade after decade.

"It's going to take some work, but I think we can make it fun, too, if we tackle it as a team. What do you think?"

I watch my staff glance around at each other, cautiously smiling and nodding.

"Hey, count us in," says Paul.

"Excellent! Our first project is going to be producing an ongoing, quality monthly newsletter. My awesome wife has volunteered to spearhead the content for this project, and she's going to handle getting at least the first few issues off the ground for us, beginning today.

"We have just over three weeks until the first of next month, so we need to hustle if we want it out by then. So Cindy will be calling each of you this afternoon for a short, exploratory phone meeting."

"Um, what are we going to explore?" Mindy looks baffled.

"*You*. Your interests. Your unique skills. I know you all have passions and talents that you don't get a chance to use every day on the job here. Well, we're going to start using them. Heck, we're going to start *celebrating* them!"

Beth inquires, "How, exactly?"

"Well, this is what I'm thinking, guys…"

HOW TO GET MORE PROFIT

1. SELL TO NEW CUSTOMERS

2. SELL TO EXISTING CUSTOMERS

3. RETAIN CUSTOMERS LONGER

We've found that most agencies don't have a good grasp of their true customer acquisition costs when we begin working with them. This is also a common issue for small business owners, in general.

And we get it – you may just want to focus on talking to your customers and selling insurance. That's what you're good at. Analytics and marketing are probably outside of your comfort zone.

With that said, please take the time to follow Jim's lead and run your own numbers. It's important to know where you've been, where you are, and where you're heading. It's the only way to really know what's working, what isn't, and how to best allocate your precious resources of money, time and effort.

There are three vital Profit Levers your agency needs to keep front and center at all times:

1. Sell to new customers
2. Sell more to existing customers
3. Retain customers longer

A quality monthly publication can help you do all three more effectively.

Monthly newsletter/publication marketing offers you a unique opportunity to connect one-on-one with people on a regular basis, which is why it remains so popular. But, if you're not going to commit to sending the newsletter out via mail or digitally, every single month for the long term, then don't bother starting.

Feeling overwhelmed?

Take a good, long look around you. No man (or woman) is an island. You have a built-in support system of family, friends and employees.

A huge mistake small business owners typically make is thinking they need to do everything themselves. It's an impossible feat, one which will doom you to certain failure.

You can hire someone to handle your newsletter or it may be possible to keep everything in-house, at least initially, if you're on a very tight budget. If you honestly feel you and your staff have some of the necessary expertise, it can be a team-building exercise. With that said, it can also be a disaster, so proceed cautiously.

Your newsletter is the perfect place to spotlight your employees in order to make your customers feel like they're getting to know you, and that they're part of your family. Do a little bio or interview with a different employee every month. Include their photo and some personal information.

Because you *must* get personal.

The more your clients see you as *people*, and the more they feel like a part of your group, the harder it becomes to leave your agency because some guy down the street or on the internet can save them a few bucks.

Success in providing insurance and financial services depends heavily upon the relationship and trust that you develop with clients and the community you serve. Become their trusted advisor.

Optimize your newsletter's reach by integrating it with your website and archiving all issues, so that prospects are able to see the great value-added services you provide for your customers.

Sound like a lot of work? Maybe.

But trust us, friend, this effort will not be wasted. It will, in fact, become one of the key marketing pieces that propels your agency toward true success.

At AMM, we make our clients the publisher of their own digital monthly magazine for the community in which the agency serves.

The magazine furthers their trusted advisor status in customers' eyes. We also ship print copies of the magazine to the agency and mail them to customers, as options.

Each full-color issue contains 128 custom components, making it truly personalized to each client's agency and staff. Every magazine includes fun, timely and seasonal articles, recipes, book reviews, local events, information on business partners and other cool things most folks would be interested in, written by our staff of professional copywriters.

We also like to throw in little puzzle contests and giveaways our clients may be conducting. People love to win stuff! And it engages them, right? Then, instead of the publication being a passive exercise (reading), it actually makes the customers active participants, as well as keeping them looking forward to the next month's issue.

We do all the work for our client agencies, and they get all the glory. Good deal, right?

We encourage you to truly commit to implementing this little jewel of the marketing world for your own agency, and make a pledge deep in your heart to put a newsletter out once every month, without fail. Your customers will begin to look forward to it over time and it will help you to be seen as an industry leader, building your credibility.

We highly recommend hiring a professional proofreader if you can afford it. If not, everyone on your staff needs to proofread each newsletter before it's sent out. Please don't trust spellcheck to catch everything. This is your *brand*, your *reputation*, and it must be a quality publication.

Watch closely for:

- Poor sentence structure
- Improper grammar, typos and punctuation
- Poorly reproduced images

Once you're satisfied that you have a clean, quality publication on your hands …voila!

You have a thoughtful, meaningful, touch point into your clients' lives on a consistent basis.

Cool, right?

Our friend Jim seems to have a handle on his newsletter and may finally be beginning to see the light at the end of the tunnel. That's great. But he still has a lot of issues to deal with, as we saw at the beginning of the chapter.

Pssst…

In a couple of chapters, we're going to share another piece of the equation which will take your publication to an off-the-charts place in marketing effectiveness, *greatly* enhancing your reputation and credibility in the community and, ultimately, bringing in *many* new customers simply by word of mouth.

And will it help customer retention? Oh, yes, so hang on tight!

*Get ideas for your agency's own newsletter and check out some of the monthly magazine AMM publishes for clients here: www.AgentsOfChangebook.com/resources.

CHAPTER FIVE
IS THAT A LIGHT AT THE END OF THE TUNNEL OR JUST AN ONCOMING TRAIN?

That afternoon, I speak with one of the graphic designers Vince recommended. We review the concepts Cindy and I came up with for the magazine, and the designer is very helpful. She even contributed some great suggestions for me to consider.

Together, we reach a working plan: I will provide her with the content for the digital magazine each month, she will send the completed publication to me for my approval, and then send it on to the printer – all for only $300.

The printer will then provide me with 100 copies just to give to the new customers and prospects we meet with throughout the month. Everyone else will receive the magazine digitally.

I'm feeling good about this plan – it not only feels like the best of all worlds, but it's something I can actually afford.

'Copywriter' isn't an entirely new role for me, as I've occasionally written blog posts for the Wakefield Insurance website, but getting the rest of the content finalized isn't easy given the continuing drama going on in the office.

Since I can't simply hit the 'pause' button on regular business, or on the fires I still have to put out each and every day, it takes until the first of the following month to produce our first issue – a month longer than I had hoped.

However, everyone has maintained their excitement about their own 'pieces parts', as well as the idea of doing all of this to build relationships with our customers. Cindy proves to be a real Godsend, keeping us on target and encouraging us all to put personality and fun into each article. And she has a lot of great ideas of her own.

My wife is indeed a marvel! Thank goodness we're back on the same page and some of the pressure is off at home. Cindy and I have shared some wonderful talks lately, and Kenzie has joined us for a few enjoyable family outings that have been exactly what I needed to take the pressure off and recharge my batteries.

I really have to remember that equation in the future…

Happy family time = Happy life + less stress

It takes a little while, but Mindy and I work together to figure out how to use our system to email the magazine to our contact list. We include Vince as a prospect so he'll receive it, too. We haven't spoken in almost two months – I've simply been too busy. Like a little schoolgirl, I'm on pins and needles to see Vince's reaction to my new baby.

As I watch my very first community magazine be sent off into the ether of the internet, I breathe a sigh of relief. Finally! Hope blossoms in my heart as a smile spreads across my face. I'm just *sure* this is going to be what we need to bring in more business and enhance customer retention.

And then for the next two hours, I watch my inbox fill up…and up…and up with magazine un-deliverable emails bouncing back to me.

Bad email addresses. Shoot!

What a buzz kill.

I beat the staff up a little bit about accurately recording customer emails, and labor the rest of the afternoon, calling each customer personally to get the correct addresses. Grrrr. What a waste of time. And I still haven't heard from Vince.

Toward the end of the day, my cell phone finally rings. It's Vince.

"Man, you did it! Congrats, Jim! It looks great. I'm really impressed at what you pulled together. Listen, I'm about to board a plane for Brazil, so I've only got a few minutes. But when I get back, let's get together on some new ideas."

"Excellent, Vince. I'm so glad you liked the magazine!"

"So how's the website doing for you?"

Luckily, I've just gotten my Google Analytics reports, so know the answer off the top of my head. "Not great. We had 88 unique visitors. But I figure those are most likely the new customers with whom we reviewed the website while on the phone, as well as them clicking on the links from our follow-up 'Welcome' email."

"Well, that kinda sucks, man. How many contacts did you email the magazine to?"

"About 1,500 that were good email addresses."

"You know, Jim, another option is to just email them some teaser copy with a nice graphic, and have them click on a link in order to view the entire magazine on your website. That would train your customers to utilize your website and see all the other cool stuff you have on there."

"Yeah, that's a good idea." I don't really think I have that much cool stuff on the website, but I make a mental note to pursue it at a later date.

"Another quick thought – in the next issue, why don't you include a big shout-out of thanks to everyone who recommended your agency?"

"Um…recommended?"

"You know – referred. It's the same thing, but I've found over the years that people don't put their guard up so much when they're asked to *recommend* a business. I mean, we all like to recommend good things to our friends, right?"

"Gotcha. Yeah, I guess we could do that. I already sent all 5 of those customers a $10 gift card, too."

Vince is silent for a long moment.

"Vince? You still there?"

"*Whoa*...you mean to tell me you only got 5 recommendations last month? For real? You have over *1,000* customers...and got 5?? Man, oh, man. That's not good.

"Ooops. Sorry, Jim, they're calling my flight. But seriously – you need to work on that process, *now*, buddy. Cause it's broken." He cackles. "Are you *sure* people even like you, dude?!"

I have to laugh as I get off the phone. Vince can act like such a jackass, and he's always so proud of it – he wears it like a badge of honor.

Then I start thinking. Process? What process? People either give us referrals – recommendations – or they don't, right?

I'm always reminding my agents to *ask* for them, but I know that's something that usually slips through the cracks.

Even I'm guilty of that.

Time to go back into research mode. I call Cindy to tell her I'm going to be a little late and spend the next hour checking our stats on referrals.

Moving to the whiteboard, I start recording some of the information so that I can study it. In doing the numbers, I find that the prospects coming to us from a referral have an average closing rate of 65%.

Very cool.

The sample size is quite small, and I'm not sure if it'll hold up since those are mostly people who have called in due to another customer referring them – as opposed to my staff actually *asking* for the recommendations.

But even so…even if it's only 50%, that still buries all my other lead sources by a *mile*. For leads that I purchase, the closing rate is only somewhere between 2 and 10%.

If each of our 1,000 customers provided just 2 recommendations, I could conceivably *double* my book.

Surely, that isn't realistic. But still, why shouldn't that be the goal? Why have I been settling for a lousy 5 a month?

Continuing my scrawls, I move to a clean spot on the board and draw 5 people across the top – me and my 4 employees.

Then under each stick figure, I write our goal for the number recommendations each of us should achieve. I end up figuring that the goal should be the same for each person since all of us have many opportunities each day to get them.

20 recommendations per person is just 1 per day, and it totals a nice round 100 per month. After choosing a conservative closing rate of 50%, we're looking at 50 new customers due to recommendations per month.

Wow! That's more customers than we've been getting from all sources *combined* every month.

The ever-present thorn in my side…that I've been beating myself up about for *months*…the profit trigger I had been hoping Vince would hand to me on a silver platter…was how to bring in more customers. And here, finally, is the answer.

Sell more to new prospects *through recommendations*.

As soon as I get to the office the next morning, I fly onto the internet and read everything I can find about referrals. Apparently, no one else has caught onto Vince's pet term – recommendations – but the explanation he'd given of why he uses the term makes a lot of sense, and I'm going to stick with it. And train my people to begin using it, too.

It seems that a 50% or better closing rate for referral leads is very common, regardless of the industry. I find one study that had supported a 62% average closing rate.

Now, if I could just figure out how to get *more* recommendations.

My reading suggests that there needs to be an emphatic 'culture of referrals' within the business. The entire agency, and our customers as well, need to know that this is something of great importance and that recommendations are *expected*; that they are the norm.

Excitedly, I draw up an Action Plan on my whiteboard.

I spend the next couple of weeks carrying out my Action Plan, adding items to it as I get new ideas.

I pay my graphic designer $75 to design a sign for the reception area spotlighting the agency's new Customer Rewards Program. It looks great. And I add a whole new section on the program to the next issue of our magazine.

Patting myself on the back, I sit back and wait for the recommendations to roll in, turning my mind to dealing with everything else currently on my plate.

At home, things are busy, too. Every night over dinner the girls regale me with tales of the big fundraiser Kenzie's taking part in. She and Eddie are on a community soccer team, which is selling magazines to buy new uniforms and equipment. Starting out by going door-to-door, they sell some magazines, but my daughter has bigger plans. And as I know by now, my girls are pretty strong-willed and creative.

After the third day of door knocking, Cindy and Margie are sitting with the kids brainstorming over milk and cookies how they might sell more magazines. Kenzie is relaying how Mrs. McCabe down the street told her to go two blocks down and tell another neighbor that Mrs. McCabe said she should buy a subscription.

That gives Cindy an idea to tie the fundraiser in with her new pet project. She and Margie have been helping out at the local homeless shelter a couple of days a month for the last few months. So the two moms decide that they will donate an hour serving meals at the shelter for every person who purchases a subscription and recommends another neighbor – and is willing to pave the way by texting them about it right away.

Well, amazingly enough, the response is overwhelming. Kenzie and Eddie end up selling over 40 subscriptions to our neighbors, half of whom are willing to text a friend, and most of those also pitch in to help.

The kids are over the moon excited, because they raised a bunch of money for their team and the neighbors seemed so excited to be helping out both the kids and the homeless shelter. A win-win! And it looks like Cindy and Margie will be busy volunteering extra hours for the foreseeable future.

When the fundraiser is finally put to bed at the end of the month, we go over to the Kingstons for a family pizza and game night. Kevin and I are so proud of our wives and kids!

And I love how what I'm doing at the office is fueling what happens at home, and visa versa. I really can't wait to see how going after recommendations will turn out for the agency.

WAKEFIELD TEAM
(FOR NOW)

20   20   20   20   20

TOTAL RECOMMENDATIONS = 100

x 50% CLOSING

50 NEW
   CUSTOMERS
      PER MONTH!

The next month, I anxiously sit down to review the agency analytics.

The final number of recommendations: 10.

Not 10 recommendations per staff member – 10 recommendations total for the agency.

The entire team only achieved half of the goal I set for each individual team member!

My first reaction is anger at the staff until I remember that I myself only brought in 4 myself. Damn. As the owner, shouldn't I be waving the flag and leading the charge?

Sitting back in my chair, I try to determine why I myself failed so miserably. Is it possible that, as the owner, I feel like I'm above asking for recommendations?

Does it feel too salesy?

Or did I just forget?

If I'm being brutally honest with myself, probably a little bit of each of those.

I recall that at the beginning of the month, I'd asked pretty much everyone I spoke to. Most of them had said they'd think about it and get back to me. Of course, they never did. And then my efforts had just kind of…fizzled.

Another thing that bothers me is that offering a $10 gift card feels kind of…dumb. Flimsy. What can anybody do with $10? That's nothing to get excited about; nothing to go out of your way to get.

I mean, we're asking a lot of a valued customer…

First they need to provide us with the name and phone number of a friend or family member.

Next they need to contact the people they referred to let them know why in the world they passed along their name to an insurance agency.

Finally, our customer needs to ask their family or friends to get a quotation on a policy.

And what's in it for the referred friend – oops, recommended friend – for letting us quote them?

Zip.

They don't even get the gift card or a drawing entry! And if the customer hasn't called them first to warm them up, it's essentially no better than a cold call.

I sigh. Maybe an insurance agency is just a different animal. After all, we have limits on the amount of money we're allowed to pay for each recommendation, at least in our state.

And who the heck really wants a $10 gift card? They're kind of a pain. I know that I can't stand carrying the darned things around in my wallet, taking up precious real estate. Remembering to *use* them is a whole other challenge.

And you rarely get the full value, because when they're down to under $2, who's going to keep hauling them around? Everybody just pitches them.

I'd bet at least 20% of the value of gift cards never gets used, or the card gets lost before it is every used even once – but the companies that sell them get all of their money up front. That's a nice extra profit for those businesses, but it's not helping me at all.

Glancing at the whiteboard, I see my Customer Lifetime Value staring back at me.

$1,388

I'd be willing to spend some big money to get recommendations that would close at 50% or more. Oh, yeah.

When I buy leads, I pay up to $20 each and only about 2% become customers. That's hundreds of dollars a month I've spent, *thousands* of dollars over a year, for very very little return on my investment because the leads are garbage.

On the other hand, I've proven that the customers we've brought in from recommendations purchase more policies, have a longer lifetime with the agency, and are more likely to recommend others to us.

Shoot, if I could just figure out how to do it, in an absolutely-and-completely-legal-and-no-threat-to-my-license sort of way, I'd be willing to pay up to $200 for leads like that.

But how the heck do I go about getting more recommendations when both customer and employee resistance seems so high?

Ahh, the siren call of the ever-elusive recommendation.

Anyone who's been in business for longer than a few months, or who has done any reading at all, knows that obtaining recommendations is *by far* the most effective method of lead generation.

Why? Because, just as Jim discovered, recommendations have a remarkably high closing rate versus that of other methods – 65% closing for recommendations vs. 2-10% for other lead sources.

In the previous chapter when Jim was calculating his agency's numbers, he found that the cost to acquire a new customer from purchased internet leads was $1,000 per new customer.

Using the same calculation, the cost for Jim to acquire a new customer from a recommendation will be only about $24 per new customer. This is even based on a more conservative 50% closing rate on recommendations.

Of course, the difference in these two costs is *huge,* and Jim is right to put significant focus into increasing the number of recommendations his agency receives.

Not only are customers developed through recommendations less costly, they also have significantly higher retention, averaging 93% for insurance agencies, from our research.

Aggressively pursuing recommendations is by far the best option for acquiring new customers. In fact, it's pretty much a no-brainer:

less work, less time, less money; generating greater trust, loyalty and retention.

All of the above means more profit to put in your pocket.

*View an interesting infographic comparing lead sources at
www.AgentsOfChangebook.com/resources.*

Now check this out...

➢ A Texas Tech University marketing study found that 83% of consumers are willing to refer after a positive experience...yet only 7% are asked.

So why aren't we asking every time, all the time???

At AMM, we study this very closely, and have conducted a survey to find out why agencies don't get more leads from referrals. The following were the top reasons that agency owners stated:

Survey Results

Reason #1: They don't ask, because they don't remember to ask

Reason #2: They don't ask, because they don't know how to ask effectively

Reason#3: They don't ask, because they think they've already taken too much of the customer's time

Reason#4: They don't ask, because they feel they already sold them something and don't want to ask for something additional

Reason#5: They don't ask, because they think they don't deserve to get referred or are embarrassed to ask

Reason #6: They don't ask, because when they did in the past it didn't get good results

Reason#7: They don't ask, because they think there is not a big enough incentive for customer to provide a referral

Reason#8: They ask, but customers are unwilling to provide them at the time

The survey also found that the number of referrals per staff member per month was only 2.27 (median). This number *should* be 6-10 per staff member per month for agencies that have an effective process.

Across the board, insurance agents are notoriously bad at asking for recommendations. We've found that even agents with hard-sell personalities, who basically balk at *nothing*, still feel don't consistently ask for recommendations.

Since there any so many reasons why more recommendations aren't received, the only way to combat it is with a significant and intentional culture change.

So how can you evolve your agency's culture into a Culture of Recommendations? Jim has a good start on it; all of the things that he's done so far have real value, so we suggest employing them. But that's only the beginning.

Retention and recommendations go hand-in-hand. Without both, your agency is doomed to simply limp along, a dim shadow of all it could be. With both, you will be able to build the foundation of a successful, self-sustaining business.

Things are moving in the right direction at Wakefield Insurance, but Jim needs that special something that will take his magazine, and his entire marketing program, into the stratosphere. Something that will cement his reputation and credibility, and bring in a multitude of new customers with far greater retention.

Get ready, because here it comes.

CHAPTER SIX
WHAT GOES AROUND, COMES AROUND

As soon as I walk into the office one morning several days later, my cell phone rings. It's Vince.

"Hey, Jim! Sorry about not getting back to you sooner, but I've been traveling quite a bit. I'm actually in town now for a couple of upcoming meetings."

"No problem, Vince. Were you traveling anywhere interesting?" I couldn't remember the last time I went anywhere fun for business.

"Well, if I have to sit on stage with a bunch of folks asking a million questions, it sure doesn't hurt to be in Rio! And Chicago was...windy!" He laughs. "So how's it goin' with you? Any progress with the stuff we talked about last time?"

I quickly fill him in on everything I've learned about recommendations and the procedures I've implemented, as well as my frustration with the results.

"Well, kudos, man – at least you know exactly where you stand now, and where you need to be. That's half the battle. Recommendations are *always* the way to go and pretty much everything you do – and I mean *everything* – should revolve around that."

"You free for lunch while you're here? I thought maybe we could throw some ideas around."

"Yeah, cool. Today is fairly open for me, so how 'bout the diner at 1:30?"

"See you then."

I sit down at our usual table and have an ice tea as I wait for Vince to arrive. My mind wanders as I consider my most recent hurdle.

Vince arrives a short time later, and after ordering our sandwiches, Vince says, "Hey, I didn't see the 'thank you' in your last magazine issue for the folks that made recommendations last month."

"Yeah, I was in such a rush to add the Rewards Program for customer recommendations that I kind of forgot to thank the customers who already helped us out. I'll be sure to put something in next month."

We chit chat for a few minutes, until our food arrives. Then I bring the conversation back around to my current dilemma, asking, "So, what do you think of the $10 gift card we give customers for each recommendation? You think that's lame?"

Vince swallows a bite of his Reuben before replying, "Well, yeah, it's not a big motivator, I agree. What you need is a way to make your agents *want* to ask for recommendations that will also make your customers *eager* to give them – lots of them."

Wondering if Vince is being delusional, I sputter, "Does such a creature even exist?"

"Well, I've been giving it some thought and…yeah. I think it does. I was reading a study last month about the deep personal satisfaction people get from giving to charity and helping others."

"How does that apply to me?"

"Have you ever heard of Worthy Cause Marketing?"

"Doesn't ring a bell."

"I've been aware of it for awhile, but in my opinion, it's been kinda slow to take off mostly because small businesses don't see the full potential and haven't figured out how to use it as an effective marketing strategy. Large companies, many of the most respected and profitable ones, have been incorporating it into their business strategies for years.

"Lemme ask you this, Jim: When we were in school, I know you were always out to change the world. Do you do anything now to give back to the community?"

"Sure. I mean, I'm as active as I can be. We sponsor a Little League team and I would love to coach Kenzie's soccer someday, but just can't seem to get the time. We helped to build a playground in that nice park down the street. We collect Toys for Tots at Christmas. Miscellaneous stuff here and there."

"All good. I'm not surprised. But do you have any kind of a *plan*? I mean, do you do anything on a consistent basis?"

"No. No plan. I just do it when something good presents itself."

"Sure, that's what most companies do," Vince says, nodding.

I go on, "I'd like to do more – a *lot* more, truth be told. But with everything else going on…and funds being so tight…I don't know. Everything else just seems like a bigger priority."

"Yeah I get that, dude. But what if we were to craft a whole strategy around Cause Marketing, by finding local nonprofits you could help out? Here, take a look at this research I found."

I scan the sheet of paper Vince passes to me. Part of it is highlighted:

Global CSR Study, CONE Communications/ebiquity, January 2015

Survey results found that when a company supports a social or environmental cause:

- 91% likely to have a positive image
- 87% more willing to trust
- 87% more loyalty towards that business
- **91% state they would switch brands to support a cause**

My eyebrows shoot up. "Well, this is *very* cool."

Vince smiled and got more excited, "Yeah. It is. One of the frustrations you've mentioned in the past is that competitor of yours who's nailing you with their 'lowest-price' media blitz right now, and you're losing so many clients because people will always go for saving a few bucks. And that's certainly true if they feel no loyalty to their current agency."

I nod.

"So when you think of the insurance you sell as a commodity, a lower price will win out every time, right? *But* – what if that weren't always true? Flip the page over, my friend, and take a look at the back," Vince continued.

I turn to the back and see stats from a 2014 Neilson study. It had actually found that 55% of consumers would pay more for products from brands that support causes!

"This is incredible, Vince!"

"I thought you'd like that."

"Geez, this could be a real game changer for me. Now I just have to figure out how to make this work for my agency."

"I always said you were a bright guy, Jim! Why don't you stew on developing a Community Cause Program for a few days and let me know what you come up with?"

"You know, this actually reminds me of the soccer fundraiser Kenzie and Eddie just got done with. They tied it into volunteer hours at the homeless shelter, and that's when it really took off. And the same with her Girl Scout troop selling cookies a couple of months ago. They sold tons of them! They're kind of expensive, but everybody buys them because it helps out the local kids."

"Exactly! And man, I can sure put away those cookies! She always hits me up for a good half dozen boxes."

"That's because you're a sucker, Vince!"

"Guilty as charged, man. I love a good cause. And, of course, Kenzie!"

We both laugh.

I spend the afternoon researching Worthy Cause Marketing and although there isn't a ton of information available, I get more and more excited at the idea.

My excitement is short-lived, however, as I soon find out that I have no internet connection. The hope that it's only *my* problem is dashed when I hear a scream from Mindy that she's also got nothing.

Our switch to a VOIP phone system certainly had its advantages, but now when our internet is down, so are our phones. I'm really not the most technical guy when it comes to IT problems, but this is also one of the many hats I now find myself wearing.

I walk around the office to see if any meetings were cut short.

Since it looks like it's nothing anyone at the agency did to produce the issue, I try to find the phone number of our internet service provider and sit on hold after dialing them on my cell phone.

I'm afraid that this will be everyone's excuse now for not hitting their weekly goals.

At the end of business hours, internet service is miraculously regained.

I just shake my head and decide I should go head home myself. At least I don't have to worry about this problem over the weekend, and maybe I can enjoy myself a little.

However, when I arrive home for dinner, I find Cindy in tears at the kitchen table.

Alarmed, I say, "Honey, what's wrong?!"

"I'm so glad you're home," Cindy cries. "Margie called. It's bad, Jim!" She blows her nose and continues, "I can't believe this is happening just when things were going so well!"

"Oh, my God. Is it Kevin?" I fall into a chair, terrified for my friend.

"No, it's little Eddie! He has brain cancer!" She's sobbing freely, now.

"*Damn.*" My eyes tear up as I squeeze my wife's hand.

"I sent Kenzie next door to play – I didn't want her to see me fall apart and I have no idea how to tell her. Eddie's like a brother to her! Margie is devastated and you know that Kevin loves that little boy like he's his own."

Fresh sobs wrack her body. "Margie is *completely* panicked. She would take a bullet for that child; he's all she has left of her first husband.

"And I can't even imagine the stress this is going to put on their new marriage. You know Margie is going to have to take a *lot* of time off of work to get Eddie through this, and maybe Kevin will, too. To top it all off, they've been helping out with the nursing home bills for Kev's mom, so they don't have much money left at the end of every month as it is. Their portion of the medical expenses is going to be astronomical! With no savings, what are they going to do?"

"Babe, I just don't know."

"Jim, there has to be *something* we can do. Some way to help them. Maybe rally other friends to pitch in somehow."

"Actually, honey..." I think for a minute. "Maybe we *can* help. Come on; let me pour us a glass of wine. There was something I wanted to bounce off you tonight, anyway, and I think...just maybe...it could help Kev and Margie, too."

After talking it over for an hour, Kenzie comes home from the neighbor's house, and we all made a quick dinner together. Telling Kenzie about Eddie, her very best friend, is an experience the like of which we never want to have again. We try our best to be gentle, but there's just no good way to deliver news like that. Especially to a kid.

I clean up the kitchen as Cindy helps Kenzie with her bath, and all I can think about is how lucky I am. The three of us are healthy and happy. There are so many others out there who can't say that.

Time to stop wishing and *just do it*. Maybe I can't change the whole world, but I can certainly help out those in my little corner of it. Isn't that what life is all about, anyway?

The evenings can still be chilly in Ohio at this time of year, so thinking that we could use a little comfort, I build a small fire in the living room fireplace. After teaming up to read Kenzie a story, tucking her in and kissing her goodnight, Cindy and I curl up in front of the fire.

Sipping another glass of wine, we quietly, albeit somewhat sadly, celebrate our family's great good fortune. Yes indeed – family, friends, good health and helping others – that's what life is all about.

First thing next morning, I reach out to Kevin. Telling him to put me on speaker so that Margie can hear, too, I offer my love and support. Then I tell them about Wakefield Insurance's new Community Cause Program and ask permission to use them for our inaugural fundraising campaign.

They readily agree, with many words of thanks. Through tears of gratitude, Margie says, "God bless you, Jim."

"Hey, guys, you have to understand that I have *no* idea how much money the initiative might or might not raise. But I'd like to give it a try and see what happens."

Kevin says, "We get it, Jim. Just the fact that you want to do this for us blows us away. We can't thank you enough!"

Getting off the phone, I call Vince to fill him in on the situation.

"Damn. That's a real blow. I had dinner at their house just last month, and they were all so happy with their new life together. And Eddie – man, he's a terrific little kid."

"Yeah, I know. He and Kenzie are inseparable. It's a totally awful situation. But I thought there might be something we could do to help. I came up with an idea to use them as our first worthy cause."

"Man, that's an *awesome* idea! Great thinking, Jim! Lemme know if there's anything at all I can do to help."

"I will. It sounds like they're going to be taking Eddie over to the big cancer center two or three times a week for a while, and that's over an hour each way. So Cindy's already calling around to her and Margie's group of friends.

"She thought instead of everyone taking food and stuff over willy-nilly, they could get a schedule organized. That way, they'll rotate the responsibility of taking a complete home-cooked meal over at least on the nights they have the appointments, and, you know, set the table pretty and light candles. Maybe get them to relax a little bit and enjoy a nice family dinner while they put the day behind them.

"She's also hoping to split up babysitting duty among the girls so that Kev and Margie can get a night out together once in awhile – maybe take some of the pressure off."

"Cool, man. Cindy's the best."

"Yep, out of my league for sure," I add before Vince gets the chance.

By Monday afternoon I find some time to begin instituting some of the items Cindy and I brainstormed over the weekend. I love Cindy's idea of the agency contributing to the cause on our customers' behalf, so that they don't have to incur any expense at all in order to pitch in and help out our community causes.

It's a simple change of perspective, and truly a win-win all the way around.

Taking out the Action Plan I drew up last night, I draw it up on my whiteboard.

NEED TO CHANGE THINGS UP!

1. ADJUST REWARDS PROGRAM

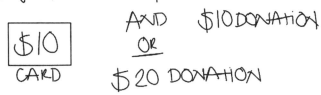

AND $10 DONATION
OR
$20 DONATION

2. HOW DO WE COLLECT?

3. GET WITH GRAPHIC DESIGNER
    - NEW ARTICLES IN MAGAZINE

4. NEW WEBSITE PAGE

5. WRITE BLOG ARTICLE

6. REVISE SCRIPT

7. MEET WITH TEAM TO ROLL OUT.

I can't wait to get going with this campaign. It feels so *good* to be doing something worthwhile!

As much as I want to help out my friends, we might even be able to raise some awareness for childhood cancer and the impact it has on families in our community. I feel like my business is just beginning to merge with *purpose*, like I've always really wanted.

Imagine you could initiate a marketing campaign that would recreate the bygone days of trust and loyalty in business. We're all nostalgic for the time of trust and compassion in the business world, aren't we? When we knew the people with whom we did business truly *cared*.

We crave relationships in this new, impersonal world. People are looking for connection, and they can still be loyal *if* we give them a good reason to be.

Worthy Cause Marketing focuses on building a reputation in your community through helping local people in their most difficult times. What exactly is it that insurance agents do, anyway? They work to protect people, to protect families.

It's a very short leap from *protecting* people, to *helping* people in need.

The United States is one of the most generous nations on earth. And we're not talking about our government. We're talking about the way our citizens dig deeply into their own pockets to help others when disaster strikes, whether in the next state or around the world.

Any salesperson's results increase when they focus on making an emotional appeal. People not only buy from people they like, they will buy *more* if you reach them on an emotional level. Worthy Cause Marketing does exactly that. It's also grassroots, produces instant gratification, is highly effective and your customers will *love* you for it.

After all, it's simply human nature to want to help people experiencing unusually trying times. At a time when most agencies, and people, are focusing on prices, appealing to emotion makes a *powerful* statement.

After all, you and your family are residents of your community. Wouldn't *you* prefer to do business with a company that was working to better the community where your children live?

In your city right now, there are guaranteed to be *countless* people in need: children fighting cancer, young families dealing with the sudden loss of their breadwinner, the elderly forced out of their homes, houses destroyed by tornadoes and flooding, battered women and children, the homeless and the hungry. The list is virtually endless.

You can be the answer to their prayers!

And one of the greatest things about Worthy Cause Marketing is that you don't even have to ask your customers for donations.

What's that?

If you don't ask customers to donate, how the heck is any money raised?

Because the agency commits to donating $10 - $20 (or more) to the cause for each recommendation they receive after the recommended person receives a quote.

So which would you really rather do: spend $10 on a Google click, which we know is largely ineffective, or contribute $10 to a local family in need, which is highly effective because it makes you stand out in your community – *and actually helps someone?*

You never knew it was so lucrative to channel your inner superhero, did you?

There are some very important reasons why this works...

1. As we've discussed, agents are notoriously terrible about asking for recommendations. Few do it on any kind of a consistent basis. But Worthy Cause Marketing gives agency team members a

different way to ask for recommendations, from each and every customer, every day.

2. The agency helps local families in need on behalf of the customer, with very little effort required from them, and zero impact on their own wallets. And by doing so, the agency is providing customers with yet another noteworthy element separating them from the competition.

3. Your community causes are guaranteed to be remembered in conversation more often by team members simply because they care about them. And for the same reason, worthy causes give customers a significant reason to provide one (or more) recommendations immediately.

4. Folks who are recommended are also more incentivized to make the effort to receive their no-obligation quote, because doing so will assist those less fortunate in their own community.

So wait...

You get more recommendations (the very best kind of lead), close more sales, enjoy greater customer retention, spend less time, build trust, develop relationships within your community, _and_ do some real good?

That's a resounding *YES.*

Pretty powerful, right?

Now, changing the habits and culture within your agency won't come easy.

In order to increase the number of recommendations consistently, we suggest you do the following:

- Brainstorm real-life client conversations where recommendations can easily be discussed.

- Develop easy, effective scripts for these situations and print them out to keep at each desk. It's much easier to ask when you know exactly what to say.
- Role-play with regularity – at least weekly. Switch roles frequently and encourage your 'customer' stand-ins to offer objections.
- Address and stress recommendations in each and every staff and sales meeting - always and forever.

We recognize that some might have the gut reaction that this type of marketing is shallow - that people in need are being used for a company's financial gain.

This train of thought is faulty. They will hopefully be able to follow this line of logic, which is undeniable:

>To grow consistently and systematically, businesses need to perform multiple marketing activities that produce new customers

>>There are costs associated with these marketing activities

>>>Marketing costs are typically paid to advertising media outlets (newspapers, websites, search engines, TV broadcasting companies, etc.), lead generation companies, printing companies, and others

>>>>If instead, some of those marketing costs are redirected to help local families and grassroots nonprofits in need, then communities are ultimately made stronger and healthier due to a local agency pitching in to help grassroots nonprofits and families in need.

There are zero negatives involved. The agency gets quality leads; customers get the satisfaction of helping others; and local nonprofits and families get the support and visibility they need.

The additional funds generated by these campaigns *would not* otherwise be raised…

No worthy cause campaign, no help outside of the norm.

And in addition, worthy cause campaigns must profit the agency or they will not be sustainable.

The very few who don't understand the logic above should simply be ignored, unless they're part of your agency team. If they *are* on your team, it's very important that they see the light and become enthusiastic about your commitment to support your agency and your community through worthy cause campaigns, or that they soon see the door.

Doing the right thing for your community is also good for business, and there's nothing wrong with that. In fact, there's everything right with it!

Keep in mind, we are not claiming that paying other sources of advertising media is bad. Many can bring value and should often be utilized in addition to or in conjunction with your worthy cause activities, as part of a complete marketing strategy.

We think that in business, for the good of all stakeholders involved, business activities should be targeted to improve the long-term profit and stability of the business. Donations or gifts generated from worthy cause activities are most easily classified as marketing costs, directly reducing profit.

As individual members of the community, donating to charities and volunteering for community associations might also be something agency owners choose to do on their own time. Donations to 501(c)(3) charities in these instances would appear on personal tax returns (unless maximum limits have been reached).

So, are you on board that Worthy Cause Marketing could take your agency to the next level? Excellent!

There are several moving parts to creating a program that works well for everyone involved, so like most large tasks, organization is key. The initiatives need to work well for your agency, your staff, your customers, your community and most of all, for the beneficiaries of your campaigns.

In short, in order to be most effective for your agency, your Worthy Cause Marketing effort needs to accomplish the following:

- Generate recommendations
- Increase agency revenue
- Promote your selected charity with exposure, donations and new volunteers
- Build your reputation as a trusted advisor in the community

Campaigns need to be well thought out ahead of time and executed according to plan, and we recommend following our highly successful blueprint.

Download our worthy cause campaign blueprint at www.AgentsOfChangebook.com/resources.

Time to check back in with Jim and see if Wakefield Insurance is experiencing any growing pains.

CHAPTER SEVEN
TO BE OR NOT TO BE A SOCIAL BUTTERFLY

The next month, I'm once again reviewing our analytics. Things are *definitely* moving in the right direction. Not as fast (or as far) as I might have liked, but the agency is approaching somewhat firmer ground than we've been treading for almost a year.

Several customers have commented on the magazine, which is gratifying to see. Response to it has been very positive and I've congratulated the staff on a job well done.

While I'm not ready to crack the cork on the champagne just yet, so far the Community Cause Program seems to be a success. I believe wholeheartedly in the concept and am *thrilled* to be doing something meaningful. My staff seems pleased with it, even if they perhaps haven't wholly embraced it as of yet.

Recommendations are up – still not quite up to the goal I had set, but they are obviously on the rise, which is *very* exciting. Some people, after reading about the fundraiser for Eddie in the magazine, have even made personal donations in addition to giving recommendations.

Across the board, the majority of customers and prospects we've spoken to have wanted to help Eddie's family by giving a recommendation, and some customers have even given 2 or more. But what's coolest of all is that *practically no one has chosen the $10 gift card option* – everyone wants the whole $20 to go directly to the Kingston family.

If I had needed my faith in human nature restored, that would have done it right there.

Since I'm not paying for Google pay-per-click ads anymore and am not wasting so much time following up on leads that produce essentially nothing, my staff and I no longer feel as if we're constantly spinning our wheels.

I can certainly see the change in all of us. With our frustration levels going down and the reduction of stress, we all seem to be breathing a collective sigh of relief. I know it's been pretty darn refreshing not to feel like I'm banging my head against a wall, for a change. We have activity, but it's good activity.

In fact, the absence of all that non-productive activity has given us more time and energy to pursue the recommendations we're getting – allowing more time to form the foundations of quality relationships – which are closing at a phenomenal rate.

As a result, the atmosphere around the office is more relaxed and upbeat. And we are all expecting bigger paychecks, which has enabled me to breathe a cautious sigh of relief. I surely hope my current staff is here to stay.

All good, good stuff. *Great*, actually. I'm super pleased.

And yet…

I can't help feeling impatient that we just aren't raising the kind of money for Kevin and Margie that I'd hoped when we started this journey a month ago. I know how much my friends are hurting, and don't want them wracked with worry over how to pay the bills when they should be concentrating all their efforts on their family and on getting Eddie healthy.

As luck or divine providence would have it, I hear the bell ring as the front door is opened. After Mindy's warm greeting, I detect a familiar voice and stride quickly to the lobby.

There stand Kevin, Margie and Eddie.

"The Kingston Trio! What a surprise! Hey, Eddie, how you feeling, buddy?" Thin, pale face, huge eyes with dark circles; it's apparent that the boy is very ill. Even so, his eyes light up when he sees me.

"I'm OK, Mr. Wakefield. How's Kenzie?"

"She's looking forward to coming over to your house tomorrow to hang out. She says she's gonna whoop you at X-Box."

"Well, she can sure try," Eddie answers, smiling.

"So guys, what's up?"

Apparently, Mindy messaged everybody, because the staff has been filtering into the lobby as we've been speaking.

Kevin says, "Well, we just wanted to come by and thank you guys for the campaign. Can we meet everybody?"

I make the introductions, while Kevin, Margie and Eddie shake everyone's hand in turn. To every staff member, Eddie says, "Thank you for helping me get better," and gives them each a megawatt smile.

"I just wish we'd been able to raise more money for you guys so far," I say.

"Jim, don't even go there with me," warns Margie. "You are *trying* – and succeeding, in my book! What you raised this month will put a good dent in this little guy's medications!" She dashes away a stray tear.

Kevin says, "Guys, really, each and every one of you has our deepest thanks. Just knowing we're not alone in this has meant the world, and we just wanted to come by and let you know how much we appreciate all you're doing for us."

After a little chit-chat and hugs all around, the family leaves for home. We all watch as Eddie walks slowly to the car, Margie helping him in and buckling him up.

To my surprise, instead of going back to their offices, everyone sinks into seats in the lobby with concerned looks on their faces. Most of their eyes are glistening with unshed tears, and not just the women's.

I say, "That was something, huh? I told you – they're really wonderful people".

"Jim...wow. I knew what we were doing was worthwhile, but...," Paul is at a loss for words, something I've never seen before.

Melissa says, "That sweet little boy! He looks so awful, but that smile! And poor Kevin and Margie look exhausted."

"We *have* to find a way to help them, "states Beth. "I mean *really* help them! These stray recommendations for $20 a pop just aren't going to put a dent into their bills if they have no savings to fall back on."

"I agree. There has to be more we can do," says Baxter.

"Whoa, Secret Agent Baxter speaks! Who knew?"

"Very funny, Mel. I just think these people deserve some real effort on their behalf, is all."

I say, "OK, team, it seems we have our marching orders. Let's all think about this over the weekend, jot down any ideas we come up with, and meet up Monday morning bright and early to compare notes."

As I walk back to my office, I marvel at what a difference meeting the family has made to my staff. It's that personal connection again; building relationships really *is* what it's all about. I bet they get a whole lot more recommendations from each customer now, all because of that personal connection. I can't wait to see what they come up with for expanding the campaign.

Later in the afternoon, I give Vince a quick call just to check in.

"Jimbo, how's it goin', bud?"

"Just great, Vince. Things are definitely on the upswing, so I really appreciate you pointing me in the right direction. We've had some positive feedback on the magazine, our recommendations have been slowly on the rise, the staff is a lot happier and things really seem to be coming together – *finally*."

"That's great to hear, man. How come I hear a 'but' coming?"

"Well, the campaign for Eddie is going well…but I just feel like we're not doing enough to spread the word. We've raised *some* money, but I want to do more."

"I hear ya. Have you posted it on Facebook?"

"It's funny you should mention that. I knew the topic would come up sooner or later, and I've been kind of dreading it, like hearing the other shoe drop."

Vince laughs. "Why would you say that?"

"I don't know. I just don't get it; I'm completely out of my depth with that stuff. It's like the elephant in the room and if I'm telling the truth, kind of scary."

"Jim, Jim, Jim. Just handle it like you do everything else – put on your brainy research hat, work your magic in figuring out how to make it work for you, and just do it, man. If you have any questions I'll be here, but *you can do this*. You know, you're very creative when it comes to adapting concepts to your own best use."

"Well, geez, I guess now I really *do* have to figure it out, if you're going to be all nice about it!"

Vince is laughing as I hang up the phone.

Mindy is our Facebook person. Occasionally, I have her post things on home or auto insurance that the carriers provide. And once or twice a week, she posts little snippets with pictures, when we have them.

I would prefer to just ignore the whole thing, but I've known for awhile that I need to learn how to take greater advantage of social media. Heck, everywhere you go, people are talking about how businesses are missing the boat if they don't.

Turning to my computer, I begin researching, trying to stay away from the fluff. It doesn't take long to run across a few seemingly legit studies showing that companies are actually able to get real, measurable results from utilizing Facebook. In fact, a whole lot of top businesses use it to post interesting content, build relationships with their customer base, engage people with their website and build their prospect list.

It certainly has the potential to expand the reach of my marketing efforts, if I can just figure out how to use it to our benefit.

Because in my mind, it's got to have a return on investment. Social media *seems* free, but it really isn't. You simply *have* to factor in the man-hours required to post and manage content, because that's precious time taken away from customer and prospecting calls and the building of relationships.

But it sounds like I can tailor it exactly to my wants and needs, and I'm blown away by how minutely I can select precisely which people will be able to see my posts and ads.

Man, this could be a real goldmine.

And I pretty much thought this stuff was just for teenagers!

Sitting back to reflect for a moment on all I've learned, I feel a little embarrassed that simple fear and lack of knowledge have prevented me from using such a powerful tool – a tool which has the potential to have a *tremendous* impact on my long-term revenue through relationship building with my prospects, customers, business partners *and* the community-at-large.

Times they are a'changin', indeed.

I'm surprised and a little chagrined to see that, although somehow 122 people had 'Liked' our Facebook page, only a handful of those had even been able to see the posts we make every week. Apparently, the posts hadn't been entertaining enough for Facebook; and I guess I can understand why.

I discover that the way a social media platform works is when the broad user base thinks a post is interesting enough that multiple users comment on it or share it with others. Those posts get more people engaged in the platform, which is what the platform needs so that it can make money through advertising.

It makes sense. It is, after all, a business. It has to make money somehow.

Analyzing the handful of our agency posts that had gained traction in the past, they all seemed to be funny, motivational or mainly focused on events – in particular, a Wakefield family get-together and a school/community carnival we had sponsored. Both had cute pictures posted.

Interesting.

In fact, I saw that Melissa had posted a photo on her personal page of the agency's banner at the school carnival, along with a photo of me and Cindy with some other parent volunteers. It was shared 23 times, liked 39 times and commented on 7 times.

Through those simple activities, it had reached a total of *2,871 people*!

Hmm…that image had appeared in the timelines of 2,871 people, probably 99.9% of whom weren't even Wakefield customers. Wow! And it all started with just me, Cindy, and two employees, all sharing the photo on our personal pages.

Absolutely remarkable!

It's weird for me, a private kind of person, to really 'go social' like that. But if I want to have customers stick with us for the long-term, I'd better start fostering relationships through this medium. After all, I'm just *one* guy, and I have *thousands* of customers.

With Facebook, I can reach out to them without having to place a call, compose an email, make a personal visit or even type a text.

Within minutes, I can communicate and stay in touch with an *incredible* number of people.

Who knew?!

Time to get with the program, Jim, old boy.

OK, so I'll clean up our page a little and add Facebook sharing to the list of weekly activities for all of us. We can all start posting more frequently, not just on the Wakefield page, but on our personal pages, as well, focusing on content other people will be interested in and will want to share.

And we'll keep it personal. After all, that seems to be what speaks to people the most. Guess it's just another facet of building relationships, right? Letting folks see us as people.

The thought of building relationships reminds of the stack of birthday cards on the corner of my desk. After finally understanding that increasing my retention is going to take doing a bunch of often small activities on a consistent basis, I made the decision to mail handwritten birthday cards to customers through the good ol' U.S. Postal Service, replacing our prior policy of emailing them.

It really doesn't take too much time to just do it, and the cost is nothing compared to the $560,000 of profit that I could lose out on if I don't increase my retention. That number is one thing that has not yet been erased from my memory — or my whiteboard.

The birthday cards were one of the changes I made when implementing a process to monitor customer feelings towards the agency, and then engage them with more personal communications.

After I address the last card to one very eccentric and funny older customer, Kennedy Morgan, I pick up the stack and drop it on Mindy's desk. I feel satisfied as I turn off the lights and head home following yet another week of learning how to do things differently, and then grinding it out.

On Monday morning, the team convenes for our morning meeting. A great round-table discussion develops over how to reach more people and raise more donations for our current community cause.

"So, guys, I really appreciate the time and thought you've all put into this. I know that meeting Eddie and his parents was a real motivator, and it really just reinforces everything we've been talking about over the last few months about building relationships and making personal connections.

"Baxter, great point about creating some posts with pictures of the Kingston family on Facebook. And we can keep people up-to-date on our fundraising efforts.

"Believe it or not, boys and girls, I started stepping out of my comfort zone a few days ago and began checking into the marketing potential of social media!"

"Whoa, I guess you *can* teach an old dog new tricks," cracks Beth.

"Hey, watch who you're calling an old dog! A dinosaur might be more like it, to tell the truth. But I'm learning."

"You know, Jim," says Melissa, "I don't know how far you've taken your education, but there are online applications that'll allow us to easily schedule and track posts, and that will also post to other social media sites for us at the same time. Because while Facebook is the Big Guy, there are other sites we could utilize, too. Are you familiar with Twitter?"

"Hey, dinosaur here, remember? No, actually, I've seen some entertaining stuff from pro athletes that I like, but as far as using it myself, that's a big *no*."

Mindy pipes up, "Yeah, Boss, we could set up Twitter and Google+ too, with the same posts – same idea, just different platforms. Might extend our reach a little."

"OK, Mindy and Melissa, why don't you team up and get that done this week, and please keep me apprised. And let's make a note to keep tabs on the other sites out there and see where they're going. If we can figure out what's up-and-coming and what other businesses are using successfully, that might be to our benefit. You two will be our new Social Media Gurus."

"Oooooh, I feel so special! Don't you feel special, Mindy?" gushes Mel.

"Funny. OK, we all seem to like Cindy's idea of a rally for Eddie, too. We'll set aside an entire Friday, open our doors to the community and just focus all of our attention on raising money for our community cause.

"My family lives in a pretty tight-knit neighborhood with the Kingstons, so Cindy and I will invite all the neighbors, post an invitation on Facebook to the community-at-large and we can send email invites to our customers and prospects.

"Cindy will spearhead the initiative and the agency will sponsor it, handling pizza, salad and soda, and we'll have a couple of tables set up on the grass where people can give us recommendations in exchange for Wakefield donating to the family on their behalf."

I conclude, "Everyone can meet Eddie, Margie and Kevin, and the family will be able to bask in the out-pouring of love and support from the whole community. Maybe recharge their batteries a little for the battle ahead of them. Sound good?"

"Sounds *great*, Boss! Hey, why don't we have some tee shirts made for the staff?"

"Terrific idea, Mindy! Why don't you run with that? And let's order a banner for our new Wakefield Insurance Community Program, too, that we can use for the rally and beyond."

I head back to my office with second thoughts about putting Melanie and Melissa on the social media project. They could spend too much time on it and not get around to their other important tasks. But, I just don't have the time to research other options right now. I'll keep an eye on them.

Adding *Social Media Management* in my notebook to the list of processes that will need to be made more efficient in the future, I remind myself that it's better to take action now and see what works.

Things are really moving along for our friends at Wakefield Insurance, aren't they? Jim has been working hard to uncover all the pieces that need to align and fit together seamlessly to complete an effective marketing puzzle for his hometown agency.

Resistance to utilizing social media can be quite strong, especially among older agency owners who didn't grow up with the concept. One of your authors has a family member who, for a long time after smartphones came out, handed every new phone she bought straight to her young daughter to program for her. And the thought of Facebook was way outside of her comfort zone.

But she slowly came around, and you can, too. Mastering social media should be a crucial component in your marketing strategy moving forward.

After all, according to Mediakix:

- The average person will spend nearly two hours (approximately 116 minutes) on social media everyday
- 50% of the entire U.S. population is now on Facebook

Facebook has allowed businesses to greatly extend their efforts by opening up potential clients and business partners they would never otherwise have had the opportunity to reach so quickly and easily.

Think of it this way - your clients and prospects are online and being social *constantly* throughout the day. They need to see you there, too, being active and visible; keeping them in the loop and promoting your brand.

At AMM, we implement powerhouse social media marketing tactics by keeping our clients up-to-date with Facebook, Twitter, Google+ and YouTube videos. We post multiple times every day to give our clients the upper hand in their communities.

By posting about current community cause information, the monthly magazine, and other happenings within the agency, we engage people emotionally with our client agencies, and visibility grows exponentially as people share the posts on their own pages.

It enables large numbers of people to see that our clients are doing something radically different from all of the other agencies in their area – namely, that they are giving back and supporting their communities, and supporting local families in need of a helping hand. Their brands and reputations grow, enhancing familiarity, credibility and trust, thereby creating new loyal customers and business partners and generating more revenue.

In fact, we've found that one of the seven keys to putting your agency in the top 10% of agencies in garnering recommendations happens to be Facebook community cause post sharing by the entire team! And you'll soon discover that posts which engage people in a personal way will be the most successful.

Just like the content you develop for your magazine, focus on keeping posts fun, informative, relevant and personal. Use social media as a platform to let people get to know you and your staff and become part of your agency's family.

*Access AMM's '3 Easy Steps to Facebook Success for Insurance Agencies' recorded webinar at www.AgentsOfChangebook.com/resources.

Communicating to customers through text messages is also very effective. We make fun of it, and mostly we don't even notice it anymore, but virtually everywhere you go and everywhere you look, people are *glued* to the screens of their phones.

Text messages grab people's attention RIGHT NOW. So it just makes sense to be where your customers already are, and engage them there. No need to make it any more difficult than that.

At Wakefield Insurance, Jim found that when one of his employees posted a cute picture from an agency-sponsored event on her own personal Facebook page, the post took off, reaching almost 3,000 people. That was a terrific lesson for him to learn.

Each of your employees can and should become *Brand Ambassadors* for your agency by sharing your posts on their own pages. As we've seen, viewership will grow at tremendous rates, creating awareness of your brand throughout segments of the community you may otherwise have been unable to tap into.

Word-of-mouth marketing has long been a vital way for companies to extend the reach of their brands, and in this day and age of social media, it's even *more* important.

It's time now for our friends at Wakefield Insurance to begin spreading their brand message throughout their community by turning their attention to Public Relations.

What great timing that Jim and his staff have stumbled upon such a highly effective public relations tool: the Cause Rally Day.

Let's see what happens as they run with it. And be sure to grab some napkins, because it's pizza time!

CHAPTER EIGHT
THE IMMORTAL WORDS OF P.T. BARNUM

As I sit at my desk several days later eating my lunch, I reflect on our progress to date and feel quite encouraged.

Mindy and Mel have been hard at work on their new social media project, so that is coming along nicely. It seems social media can be a two-way street; that in addition to making posts for the agency, we can also create targeted lists of people in the community we would like to track especially closely for business purposes. We call it a 'Centers of Influence' list. Very cool.

My weekly To-Do List now includes 15 minutes twice a week to react to the posts of those on my 'Centers of Influence' list. During that time I'll review, like, comment and share the posts of people and businesses with whom I would like to develop relationships.

It's just human nature for people to keep closer tabs on those who are regularly interacting with them. I should've known – haven't I been discovering the same thing with my own customers over the last several months? It's just another facet of building relationships. It all dovetails so beautifully.

I've also been tinkering with some of the privacy settings, allowing me to feel that I still have some small degree of privacy. So all in all, I'm beginning to feel somewhat more in control of the social media beast.

As I polish off my sandwich, my mind strays to a quote from P.T. Barnum I saw only this morning as I picked up an order from the printer. It had been posted on his bulletin board:

"Without promotion, something terrible happens...nothing!"

Ain't it the truth?! All the previous month, I'd fallen into the same trap with the Community Program as I originally had with our website – *if you build it, they will come.*

How on earth are people supposed to know about the campaign (and all the other changes we're implementing) if we don't promote it throughout the community? And now with the rally coming up, it's even more important to spread the word. But how?

Mindy comes into my office to sit down for a quick chat, and I share my thoughts with her.

"You know Boss," says Mindy, "I hadn't thought of it until now, but when I worked at the PR firm before coming to Wakefield, they used to do press releases to get the word out about stuff. Couldn't *we* do a press release? Send it to the local papers?"

"That's a *great* idea, Mindy," I reply. "That never even occurred to me. Do you have any experience writing press releases, by any chance?"

"Well, yeah, actually – I do. I'm a little rusty, and I'm certainly not a professional writer, but I'd be happy to give it a go. Then maybe you could do a look-see and refine my rough draft. It might be better than nothing."

"Teamwork, I love it! Think you could have something for me by the end of the day?"

"Your wish is my command," she says as she twirls out the door.

Yes, team morale is definitely on the rise. And I've noticed that as a result, everyone seems more inclined to pitch in and help – help me, help each other and just generally do whatever is necessary. It's very refreshing.

That afternoon, after reviewing and editing Mindy's press release, I email it off to the Community Events departments of our town's two newspapers. I also post it on our website, and at Vince's suggestion, am looking into the possibilities of releasing it to internet news outlets. I'm not sure if anything will come of it, but hey, at least we will have tried.

After a great weekend with Cindy and Kenzie, which is equally divided between family activities and planning for Eddie's rally, I return to work on Monday rejuvenated and ready to go. Even Kenzie contributed to the planning by suggesting fun activities for the kids, including some simple, low-key things in which Eddie will have no trouble participating.

The whole family is pretty stoked, and the staff is, too.

It's a tremendously busy week. In addition to all of the arrangements for Friday's event, there are still recommendations to follow-up with, customer service tasks to perform, social media blurbs to post and magazine content to prepare.

Although the rally is taking up a lot of our time, if it turns out to be a success, I'm starting to think we could perhaps cookie-cutter it for other causes down the line. At the very least, it'll be a tremendous learning experience.

Cindy is handling the food and drinks, as well as picking up the tee shirts and banners Mindy ordered. I draw up the To-Do List for the staff, divvying up the various tasks.

Let's RALLY PLAN

- POST SOCIAL MEDIA REMINDERS

- SEND EMAIL REMAINDERS

- PRINT CALL PLANS

- CALL CUSTOMERS + FRIENDS FOR RECS.

- CALL CUSTOMERS FOR CROSS-SELLS

- CALL PAST CUSTOMERS FOR WIN-BACKS

- HAND OUT SCRIPTS

Rally Friday finally arrives, dawning fair and lovely – a perfect July day in every way. The team is riding high on enthusiasm as we set up in the lobby and on the front lawn, blow up balloons and start getting the food and drinks ready. The Kingston family's arrival is greeted with hugs and kisses, and they are obviously thrilled with everything the team has done.

"LOVE the shirts, Jim," sings Margie.

"Got 'em just for you, Marge – I know what a fashionista you are," I reply with a bear hug.

Later in the afternoon, Cindy and I pause in the midst of the madness to catch our breath and share a quiet moment. Looking around I ask, "Cindy, did you ever imagine in your wildest dreams we would have this kind of turnout?"

"I hoped, Jim. For our friends' sakes, I hoped. Thanks so much for doing all this, Honey!"

"Hey, the agency is making out like a bandit! People are being hugely generous, not only in personal donations but with *tons* of recommendations. A lot of people are just going straight down the contact list on their phones just because they want to help. How cool is that?"

"I've always said, do the right thing and it all comes back to you."

Vince meanders over, saying, "Awesome job, guys! You've really done something wonderful here, man. The whole community's come together and our buddies are totally grooving on all the love and support. This should help them get through what're sure to be some dark days ahead.

"Listen, there's something else I wanted to run by you for your future campaigns. But...we'll have to chat about that later because I think there's someone here who would like to talk to you," Vince says as he steps aside.

"Excuse me – are you Jim Wakefield? Of Wakefield Insurance?" I turn and see a young woman standing behind me with a notebook in hand.

"That's me!"

"I'm Carrie Jo Donaldson with the News-Gazette. And this is my photographer, Ethan Martinez. I'd love to hear about your Community Program. I wondered if I could get a few moments of your time, and a photo with your staff and the family you're raising money for – is it the Kingstons?"

We all shake hands and talk for a few minutes while Carrie Jo takes notes, then I call the team over and introduce each of them. The Kingston family joins us for a few more questions and some pictures.

On Monday morning, the team is still flying high. Seeing themselves and our worthy cause in the Sunday paper has been the icing on top of a wonderful day. It's both amazing and gratifying to see the effect that helping someone in need has made on all of them.

We spend most of the morning meeting reviewing the event, discussing what worked well and what we'll change for future campaigns. We determine that we could probably save time, money and effort in the future by simply keeping everything streamlined inside the office.

But by and large, everyone agrees that most of what we did was right-on.

And the results don't lie…

Recommendations Quoted: 61
Winback Quotes: 14
Cross-sell Quotes: 33

We're still closing sales, so I'm not sure yet what the final numbers will be, but it obviously was a *bonanza* of a day for Wakefield Insurance. The recommendations have been closing at about 70% so far. And the business we've closed already makes this by far our best month since I purchased the agency.

What is even more rewarding is that between the money contributed by the agency for recommendations, and the additional personal donations people made, it looks like we raised around $2,200 for Kevin, Margie and Eddie. There were even a couple of other local business owners who stopped in at the rally, and they pledged to make generous company donations this week, as well.

So more contributions will be coming in and the word seems to be spreading like wildfire. Our first campaign is a resounding success, and I couldn't be happier about it!

When I log onto the Wakefield website later, I find that additional recommendations and donations were made on Sunday, and even this morning, presumably after people had read about the event and the family's plight in the newspaper.

Several requests for quotes had also come in through the website over the weekend and the personal Facebook posts everyone on the staff made on Friday had unquestionably taken off, with a whole big bunch of likes and shares, and some lovely comments. Friday's rally was a home-run in every way possible.

Today is a cancer center trip for Eddie, but Kevin calls from the hospital in the afternoon, asking to be put on speakerphone so that he can thank everyone once again. We fill him in on the grand total of funds raised just between the time the rally started on Friday morning and through today, and I can tell it's a struggle for him to keep his emotions in check. The whole team wipes away tears of joy right along with him.

"God bless you all! Margie and I will keep every single one of you in our prayers."

"And listen Kev, although we've put a limit of 90 days on our community causes, your campaign page will remain on our website and we'll keep the donations page active, as well. A mention of the fundraiser with a big 'thank you' to everyone who contributed will be in the next edition of our magazine, and we'll maintain our social media campaign indefinitely if it's OK with you."

"You guys can't imagine what all of this has meant to us. 'Thank you' isn't enough, but I'll say it again anyway. Thank you all so very much. Margie says to expect a couple of her special homemade pies at the office later in the week."

As I hang up the phone, Beth says, "Jim, we need to keep this positive momentum going. So what's up next, Fearless Leader?"

"Well, now we begin planning our next community cause campaign. Trust me – this is just the beginning! You guys knocked it out of the park and I'm more proud of you than I can say."

"Can't wait to see what you have up your sleeve for us next, Boss," says Mindy.

Melissa says, "So, are you up for suggestions for our next worthy cause? Because I have a little grassroots nonprofit that I help out with occasionally. They could sure use some exposure."

"I have a group, too, Jim," says Paul. "How about we all start compiling information on possible community causes and go over them at our next planning meeting?"

"Alrighty, gang. You run with it, and I'll just sit back and let *you* do all the work for a change!"

Mock protestations of outrage follow as they return to their offices to get back to work.

I sit grinning from ear to ear when I'm interrupted by the phone ringing.

It's a blast from the past – Lou, the great new agent who left the company five or six months ago and for whom I had treasured such high hopes.

"Hello, Jim? It's Lou! Listen, I read all about what the agency has been up to in the paper on Sunday. Wow, you guys are on *fire!*"

"Hey, Lou! It's great to hear from you. Yeah, it was a terrific event and we raised a lot of money for the Kingston family. So, how have you been?"

"Well...I've been following your magazine the last few months, and keeping tabs on your website and the revamped Facebook page. And your new Community Program – *wow*. It's all pretty impressive, Jim. The truth is, it's something that I would *really* like to be a part of. Could I come over and talk to you about possibly coming back?"

"Sure, Lou. Why don't you come by the office tomorrow after lunch and we'll talk it over," I reply, attempting not to sound either condescending or excited.

Cause Rally Days like the Wakefield Insurance team put on are a terrifically valuable activity.

Not all Rally Days are like Wakefield's extravaganza, but they also don't need to be. From our experience in coordinating Rally Days for our clients, even on a smaller scale, average results are still very good and more than triple the number of quotes that occur on a typical.

During the rally, the team needs to really focus on initiating conversations involving the community cause, which should really be happening on a daily basis anyway.

The Rally Day provides a strong reminder to the team, helping them to create the *habit of making those conversations second-nature*. Also of importance, it gives customers and prospects a reason to act *now*.

No marketing segment is more powerful than Public Relations. However, when it comes to hometown insurance agencies, as an agency owner you wear that PR hat all by yourself. If you're confused by the term, you're not alone – a lot of folks are. So what exactly *is* PR?

Basically, PR is simply the methods by which you reach out to your community. It's in the name, after all – *public relations*. Your PR initiatives should exist to build and maintain your agency's positive brand image throughout the community.

Studies have shown that customers, potential customers, and other businesses' perception of your company can be highly influenced by what they see in the media. So where are we going with this?

Well, we've spent a lot of time talking about how you can make your marketing efforts vastly more impactful by instituting a Community Program based on Worthy Cause Marketing principles.

But your campaigns will go nowhere fast if no one knows about them. And since your Public Relations department most likely consists of you, perhaps with some nominal help from your staff, just exactly how are you going to spread the word?

Say hello to the tool of the PR world... the press release. A press release serves as written proof of your efforts and achievements.

An effective press release will contain a brief snapshot of your cause and explain the pertinent details of the campaign in the hope that it will be picked up as a story by local news outlet. This means you'll want to be sure the press release contains actual newsworthy material – about your agency, your Community Program and your worthy cause.

At AMM, the professional copywriters on our staff prepare press releases for each of our clients' community cause campaigns, which I'm happy to say have resulted in countless newspaper articles and radio and television spots. Our Account Managers reach out personally to coordinate interviews and the placement of stories in local media outlets, highlighting the charity campaigns to fit the media outlet's appropriate community and local interest segments.

We also distribute our press releases through a very effective news wire service, which disperses them throughout hundreds of media outlets within our clients' geographical areas. What's more, the press *loves* heroes.

You, your team and your agency will be portrayed all over town as legitimate hometown heroes, working to better the community. Community reporters picking up the stories have provided *priceless* free publicity, both for our clients' insurance agencies, as well as for the local organizations benefitting from the campaigns.

Although AMM has both PR experts and national media database at our disposal, that doesn't mean that you can't do the same on a smaller scale. Because keeping local media in the loop on your Community Program will *hugely* impact your influence and the perception of your agency among your local audience.

Changing your community causes every few months allows your agency to meet a whole brand spankin' new segments of the community rife for recommendations, quotations and new business.

Jim and friends have chosen to spotlight a private family for their first community cause. And your agency will no doubt come across individuals and families in need who you would like to help, as well. That's great for everyone, all the way around. However, when you're fundraising for a nonprofit, you can structure things a little bit differently.

Let's check back in and see what we can learn from how Jim handles their next cause.

CHAPTER NINE
IT'S A VOLUNTARY THING

Five weeks later, deeply mired in the end of the hot and sticky dog days of summer, I'm reflecting on those golden days when my team seemed to be flying high. Had it really been only a month ago? Somehow we haven't managed to keep the momentum going and I'm not quite sure what's wrong. I'm starting to fear that our first worthy cause was a one-trick pony.

We held a Cause Rally Day for our new charity last weekend, but it just wasn't the same. Granted, we poured our hearts and souls into the rally for the Kingstons, due to the personal connection we all felt. So I knew going in that the results wouldn't be quite the same. But still, something was…missing. And I can't quite put my finger on it. The recommendations just aren't flowing the way they had been.

Time to check in with Vince. We haven't spoken since Eddie's rally, except for a 'congrats' text Vince sent me afterward.

"Hey Vince, how's it going, old buddy?"

"Jim! Hey man, if I were doin' any better, I'd probably get arrested!" He guffaws loudly. "So how 'bout you?"

"Cindy and Kenzie are perfect, and everyone here is fine. Beth's out on maternity leave for awhile, so it's a little quieter around here. We've all been staying involved with Eddie, and donations are still trickling in. So it's all good."

"Cool, man. How's the new campaign?"

"It's going fine. We had our Cause Rally Day last weekend, and while it wasn't the complete blow-out the last one was, it produced some respectable results. But the sizzle just wasn't there. The team was riding so high and now, they're just kind of…I don't know…droopy."

"You're raising funds for foster kids now, aren't you?"

"Yeah, and it's a really great organization, Backpacks of Hope. Apparently most kids entering the system have fled from pretty bad situations, usually with nothing but the clothes on their backs and maybe a few belongings stuffed into a garbage bag, if you can believe it. So these guys provide them with beautiful new backpacks stuffed to the brim with all the things they'll need in the short-term: personal care & hygiene products, clean socks and underwear, PJs, books, journals, teddy bears – stuff like that."

"Well, Jim, that sounds awesome. Your staff isn't feeling it, though?"

"I mean, they know it's worthwhile. And they all want to help the kids. But, I don't know – something's missing."

"Let me ask you this: why was everyone all fired up about Eddie's cause?"

"Well, about half-way through the campaign, the family came into the office to thank everyone for our efforts on their behalf and the whole staff just kind of fell in love with them."

"Not sure how you're missing this, Jimbo: *they made a personal connection.* They began building a relationship. Right?"

I'm silent for a long moment. I finally say, "Sheesh. You know that old commercial where people smack themselves in the forehead and say, 'I could've had a V8!'?"

"Yeah. Forest for the trees, man. Forest for the trees. I wanted to talk to you a little bit about this at the rally, but we just never got the chance."

"But Vince, I'm not sure how we can go about meeting some of these kids."

"Well, you don't necessarily have to meet the *kids* to feel the personal connection and get your team to feel engaged. Why don't you guys go down and help stuff backpacks? Arrange it with the charity, so they're expecting you and, you know, go in and press the flesh. Meet the folks who were so passionate about these kids' situation that they started a whole charity effort to change their world."

"That's an awesome idea, Vince. Volunteer…yeah. Knowing my guys, they'll totally get behind that! I just hate asking for their personal time."

"So close up shop a couple of hours early on a Friday afternoon and do it then. Because volunteering will help you build deeper, more meaningful relationships with your nonprofits. And keep in mind, the more you engage your staff with these groups, the more enthusiastic they'll be, the more recommendations the agency will get and the greater the funds and exposure, both for the charity *and* for the community of people they're helping."

"Of course, you're right."

"Cool. So, how're your recommendations coming?"

"Well, better than a few months ago, but I still don't feel like we're quite there yet."

"Are you using a script?"

"Kind of."

"Lemme hear it."

I rattle off what we've been saying.

"Well, that's not bad, but it's not good either – too long, too complicated. Let me shoot you over something simpler that I think will do better for you. And you guys should be practicing over and over again, at every meeting, until you can do it in your sleep – and then keep practicing some more."

"Thanks, Vince, that'd be great."

After getting off the phone, I think about our conversation. Talk about another smack in the forehead moment. Why the heck *hadn't* I come up with an effective written script for my team? I mean, we have weekly meetings and well-documented processes for handling each and every type of interaction with our customers and prospects. We talk about how to properly position different policy types, conduct annual reviews, onboard new customers, and I've developed scripts for *all* of those situations, which we role-play regularly.

So how come this one critical area – which is of such vital importance to everything we've been trying to accomplish – I just let slip through the cracks? Talk about dropping the ball. Oh, well. I guess if I were perfect, I wouldn't need any help. Anyway, we'll correct that immediately. *Today.*

Turning my thoughts back to Vince's volunteering idea, I have concerns about closing the agency early when we're still trying to get our feet under us and build a strong foundation. If the entire team is out of the office, there will be no one available to service customers. It makes me feel a little panicky.

Heading to the whiteboard, I perform a rapid calculation:
> 4 team members x \$25 average wage x 2.5 hours = \$250

Well, that's not *too* bad.

Returning to my desk, I check the system to see how many incoming service calls we typically get on a Friday afternoon. It looks like somewhere around 8. Moving back to the board, I calculate the number of missed sales those 8 calls might translate to, based on our average. A month or so ago, we were getting so many recommendations that the number was higher, and our closing average has dropped somewhat. Currently, we're getting about 2 new customers every afternoon. Adding that to the board, I sit back down to reflect.

You know, now that I think about it, volunteering might not negatively impact sales after all. I mean, the service calls can be made up the next day, and we can amend our outgoing message to say that we're out volunteering but will return their call tomorrow.

That the office is out volunteering is actually positive PR, isn't it, that? It promotes both our brand image *and* our worthy cause.

And the volunteering will get the staff more engaged and enthusiastic. Chances are pretty good that they'll come back and get even *more* recommendations in the long run. Especially with Vince's new script. Yeah…in truth, volunteering is a *sales generating event*. How cool is that?

Smiling, I quickly cross out the 2 missed sales from my equation and look up the phone number for Elizabeth, the woman who runs Backpacks for Hope. Giving her a quick call, we chat for a few minutes and arrange for the staff to go over on Friday afternoon and volunteer from 2:30 to 5:00 or so.

I gather the troops in the conference room later in the day for a staff meeting.

"Hey guys, what would you say if we closed the office a few hours early on Friday afternoon?"

Whoops and catcalls follow my announcement.

Lou pipes up, "So what's the catch?"

"No catch. In fact, I think you're all going to like this. May I have a drum roll, please? Thank you, Paul. So here it is: we're going to go volunteer for our worthy cause, Backpacks of Hope. As a team. Meet the folks, get to know them and see what exactly it is that they're doing and why, and stuff some backpacks for them."

"Awesome, Boss!" "Cool!" "That's great!"

"Hey, I have a suggestion," says Mindy. "Why don't we take along some cupcakes or something to thank them for all they're doing for these kids?"

"Nice, idea, Mindy! Thanks for volunteering to handle that," I smile as she rolls her eyes at me. "I've also found out about a few supplies they're running low on, and am going to ask Cindy to pick some stuff up to take with us."

They all smile and nod enthusiastically.

"Now, for my second topic – asking for recommendations. I've got a new script here courtesy of my friend Vince, who you all met at the barbecue. We're going to role-play with it a little bit right now, just to get the feel of it, and then we'll be practicing it in *every single meeting* going forward. We need to be able to rattle this off in our sleep in a completely natural-sounding way.

"I think we all realize that recommendations are where it's at, and we're going to keep hammering away at them until we have waaaay too much business to handle – and then keep going!"

The Monday morning after volunteering feels like déjà vu all over again, in the best way possible. The team's excitement is once again off the charts. But this time, I detect a subtle difference.

I'd noticed after Eddie's rally that the staff seemed, well, like more of a *team*. And today, that feeling is definitely intensified. It seems that working together toward a common cause, with that cause being to help others, is a terrific bonding experience. Who knew?

"Guys, let's bring this revelry under control just long enough for me to congratulate you all on a job well done!"

"Boss, Friday was *awesome*," chirps Mindy.

Paul adds, "Those *people* were awesome! What they're doing for those kids is just incredible!"

"*You guys* were awesome," says Melissa. "I was so proud of our team, the way you all threw yourselves into the experience."

"Agreed. Good to interact about something other than business, for a change," says Baxter.

"Aren't you the big softie," teases Mel.

"I loved the story Elizabeth, the founder, told about seeing her first foster child arrive with a couple of tattered belongings in a brand new shiny black garbage bag – *supplied by the foster system!* And how she vowed to stop that degrading experience from happening to other kids," gushes Lou.

Mindy chimes in, "And the new initiatives they're starting! Fun group activities for foster families, helping them to build a supportive community together – *wow*."

I say, "Hey guys – we even received several really nice messages on our voicemail Friday afternoon from customers making service calls, who learned from our outgoing message that we were off volunteering.

"So it seems as though we've struck on a winning combination. And correct me if I'm wrong, but I'm guessing you guys want to continue volunteering together?"

"Hell, yeah!" says Paul.

"That's great! I think that going forward, we'll just change up the order of the way we do things a little bit. Let's issue a press release within the first couple of weeks of bringing each new cause onboard, and maybe volunteer earlier in the campaign to help us catch that personal connection and enthusiasm. Then do the Cause Rally Day, and keep pumping up social media every step of the way."

"Sounds perfect, Jim," says Melissa.

The next day, I'm back in research mode. Last night I told Cindy about how pumped up everyone was, and she said she remembered reading something a while back about how companies who had their employees regularly volunteer together reported greater employee satisfaction and less turnover. Since employee retention has always been a monumental concern for me, this fact really catches my attention.

Immediately jumping on the computer, I soon find that Cindy has hit the nail on the head. The stats on this stuff are just incredible. There's tons of information.

I quickly find an article talking about the business benefits of employee volunteering which cites some Gallup research[7] saying that companies who place a priority on employee engagement have significantly higher productivity, profitability and customer ratings, less turnover and absenteeism, and fewer safety incidents.

I then find something interesting on The Balance.[8] In citing the top 10 critical reasons employees quit their jobs, I see that at least a

---

[7] The Business Case for Employee Volunteer & Skills Giving Programs by Sarah Ford, March 16, 2016 - Gallup Q12 Employee Engagement Assessment

[8] TheBalance.com - Top 10 Reasons Why Employees Quit Their Jobs: A Checklist for Talent Retention by Susan M. Heathfield

few of the issues would be positively impacted by volunteering together on a regular basis:

- Bad or nonexistent relationship with boss
- Lack of relationships/friendship with co-worker
- Overall corporate culture

Additionally, almost all of the other reasons cited in the top 10 are being addressed by Wakefield's new worthy cause Community Program, which will generate recommendations, and volunteering:

- Contribution of work to the organization's business goals
- Meaningfulness of work
- Organization's financial stability
- Management's recognition of employee job performance

It's so interesting how everything works together; each piece of the puzzle fitting so harmoniously.

I'm starting to realize that all the little changes we've been making over the last 8 or 9 months are working in tandem to solve virtually *all* of my problems – employee retention and engagement, customer retention and engagement, generating more business, building a successful, self-sustaining company, enhancing the agency's reputation in the community and doing something truly worthwhile for the community.

Oh, and I can't forget the positive effect all of this has had on my personal life...my health, no more chest pains...and the happiness of my marriage and family life.

And a big bonus – no more long hours. At long last, my schedule is beginning to even out, leaving me more time and energy for both work *and* home.

I had no idea when I started this marketing journey exactly how *rewarding* it would be. Sitting at my desk with the door open, I can hear my staff enthusiastically working the phones, occasionally hollering congratulations back and forth to each other, and just generally enjoying their jobs and each other.

Yes, it's becoming a real pleasure to come to work every day. I feel more than a little emotional. It's been a long time coming. Buck up, Jim old boy, and get back to work! As luck would have it, the phone rings. It's Elizabeth, from the Backpacks charity.

"Good morning, Jim! I just wanted to thank your team again for helping out on Friday and for everything you're doing for us! I was wondering if I could get your logo and contact info to post on our humble little website. It's nothing special, and we don't get all that much traffic, but your campaign has gotten me thinking about corporate sponsors, and I'd like to spotlight you guys as our very first."

"Thanks, that's a great idea, Elizabeth! I'll shoot that right over to you as soon as we get off the phone. And I had an idea this weekend, too. We're going to be sending a press release about the campaign to the local papers and I'm checking into some other outlets to get it even greater exposure. Hopefully, we'll be able to get you a few more donors during this final leg of the campaign."

"*Wonderful!* Please let me know where you place it and I'll send an email out to our small-but-loyal donor list. Again, I can't thank you enough for all you're doing for us. We're going to able to help so many more foster kids and families because of your involvement."

"Elizabeth, it's been a true pleasure. You and your organization have been an inspiration to our team. Let's stay in touch. And if there's anything else we can do for you, please just let us know."

Yeah, life is pretty darn good right now.

After shooting Elizabeth an email with the requested info, I sit back and review our conversation. You know, I went into the current community cause handling things in pretty much the same way as I did for the Kingston family. But this isn't a private family. It's an organization.

OK, it's time to put my PR hat back on. Hey, I should have one of those cool old fedoras with a 'Press' card stuck in the brim for these occasions! I chuckle to myself. Research, of course, my friend.

Hmm…it seems that when a business is in the news about something, the value of that placement is worth three times the cost of an ad in the equivalent space. And of course, being in the news is free!

Being in the news gives businesses authority and credibility, and a press release puts businesses in the news. If our agency is in the news, it would add a little more proof of our agency's credibility within our community. Not sure why I forgot to do a press release for Elizabeth earlier, but we'll fix that right now.

Vince talked about placing press releases with a newswire service, and after doing a little more research, it seems that there are just a couple of top-tier newswire services. I access the press release Cindy and I worked on last night and update it using some of the suggestions I found on how to format good press releases.

Finally, I pay the $275 fee and am relieved when my press release is accepted. I quickly send the link to Elizabeth and Vince. Vince also mentioned that Google likes high-quality press releases and will often display them on page one whenever anyone searches for my agency's name.

That's great, but how can I *guarantee* my customers and prospects will see this nice news coverage? Wanting to make the most of it, I post the press release to our website, our Facebook page and my own personal Facebook page, as well. I then send an email to the staff asking them to do the same.

When I check back in a few minutes, I see that people are already liking my post. Very cool. My phone chimes as a text comes in. It's from Vince. 'Nicely written PR for a newbie! Now get it into the hands of local media and see if they bite – TV, newspaper, radio. Any story anywhere can only help.'

I begin to text back, but then decide a call would be much more efficient and dialed Vince's cell phone.

"Hey, I sent my last press release to the two local papers, but I was wondering how I might be able to extend the reach?" I asked.

"Well, I have my guys use the same national media database of editor and reporter contacts that the big New York PR firms use. I'll have my assistant, Caroline, send along some local contacts.

Just shoot them a nice email and attach your press release. Maybe follow-up with a phone call in a couple of days."

"Hey, that's great, Vince. Thanks a million, buddy."

"Yeah, yeah, yeah. Just keep in mind that it's not easy to get larger news outlets to bite on a story. So be sure to make the most out of any opportunity you get, man, and give it real legs any way you can – social media, your website – anything you can think of."

"No problem there. When our little News Gazette did the story for Eddie, we were so excited that we framed it and put it up in the lobby, as well as posting it on the website, Facebook and in the magazine. I'll make sure to get traction for anything we're lucky enough to have come our way."

One of our favorite quotes is paraphrased from something Gandhi once said and still resonates deeply:

Be the change you wish to see in the world

Another, more common saying which you've heard from us before, 'What goes around, comes around'. Some call it Karma. And it's true, isn't it?

Wakefield Insurance is working to help improve life in their little corner of the world, and it's beginning to come back to them in so many different and amazing ways.

The grassroots organizations you choose to help appreciate the exposure, because it results in much-needed volunteers and donors. Many of these charities will feature your agency on their website, social media posts and promote the campaign to their previous donors.

Nonprofit organizations, other businesses and countless people throughout your community will begin to take notice. It won't happen overnight, but buzz *will* grow. With every community cause, press release, Cause Rally Day, social media post and volunteer activity, you engage the community on an emotional level, *showing* them that you care.

With consistent proof of these activities, agency credibility grows, and so does your reputation as a caring, trusted advisor to the people of your community.

Building relationships on a much grander scale.

One other boon for your agency - This marketing program we've been discussing can have very favorable ramifications for your employee satisfaction and retention.

It shouldn't be a surprise that Lou wants to come back and be part of Wakefield Insurance's renaissance. With the positive team vibe and enthusiasm building within the agency, we'd be surprised if this core group of agents wasn't here to stay.

Attracting and retaining good talent is a universal challenge for small business owners. Providing meaningful volunteer opportunities will give your employees the experiences necessary to form lasting bonds; bonds which will enable them to become a unified, supportive team. It engages them with each other, with your agency, with your nonprofit organizations and with the community at-large.

Volunteering together also develops enthusiasm, loyalty, self-esteem and leads to greater job satisfaction. And greater job satisfaction leads to higher, more consistent performance and a better bottom line[9].

We've seen the positive effects of volunteering at work in our own company, because at AMM, we don't just talk the talk. Our team volunteers together on a consistent basis, and we're happy to report that the benefits we reap, both personally and professionally, are immeasurable. *People want to be inspired.*

It's a universal truth that human beings *crave* inspiration. Bogged down in the minutiae of our everyday lives, our hearts and souls yearn to be uplifted; to see and do something meaningful.

A marketing plan which includes Worthy Cause Marketing at its center is *inspiring* – to your employees, to your customers, to your prospects and to the community. And a company that closes up

---

[9] UGA Today, 'UGA study finds volunteering increases workers' job performance'. February 3, 2014

shop for a few hours every month to serve others? Well, it just doesn't get more inspiring than that.

It all comes down to pride, trust and loyalty.

Employees will want to be a part of an agency that is driven by those ideals, and will be proud to be on your staff. Customers will feel trust and loyalty, and take pride in doing business with you. Prospects will be eager to talk to you, inspired by all the positive things they've heard about your company. Not a bad calling card, huh?

Sooo… now that our friend Jim is established in the community as a 'white hat', one of the good guys, how do you think he'd feel about getting something – a great, big, fat, *huge* something… from nothing?

Intrigued? Let's go exploring.

CHAPTER TEN
SOMETHING FROM NOTHING

Driving into the office a few weeks later, I'm reflecting on how much our business has changed within the fairly short amount of time we've been concentrating on creating a worthwhile marketing program.

Our website continues to evolve and improve as we develop more interesting and relevant content. I now believe it to be one of the best to be found in our industry.

And focusing on doing good for the community is proving to be *awesome* for business. Who knew trying to change the world could be so profitable?

Only yesterday we got a call from a woman requesting a quote to replace her existing insurance policies because she had heard about our Community Program. The quote turned out to be $410 *more* per year than what she was currently paying, and before I left the house this morning, I saw an email from her saying that *she wanted to switch anyway*!

Her note said that she trusted Wakefield to handle her insurance because she had seen first-hand what our agency valued, and paying $34 more a month to support us and receive all of our value-added services was worth it. Unbelievable.

The week after stuffing backpacks with Elizabeth for Backpacks of Hope, we got a call from her husband, Marcus. He owns a small fitness business and was looking for someone trustworthy to handle his gym's insurance. It turns out that we were able to save Marcus a few dollars, but he had seemingly been ready to switch, regardless of price. He simply wanted us to handle things for him because he trusted us. I surely hope this is a new trend because we could really use some more commercial business.

Although the agency started out the previous two months somewhat slowly, by instituting a few simple changes and volunteering as a team for our cause, we'd finished from a position of strength. And this time around, I have every reason to believe that the great results are no flash-in-the-pan.

Sitting at my desk later, I review our numbers for the two months.

96 total recommendations resulting in 71 quotes. 52 of which occurred in *just* the last month.

71 x $20 = $1,420 donated by Wakefield
+ $40 in other donations
= **$1,460**

We nearly doubled our $750 goal for the community cause campaign! Elizabeth is going to be so pleased. That'll help a lot of foster kids to reclaim their dignity with her backpacks.

Although the funds were sent directly to the charity from the crowdsource funding page, we got a big dry erase check to present to Elizabeth, just to make it a little more fun and special. We plan to take a nice photo of the check presentation, and then feature it on both websites, in the magazine and on social media. Sharing that photo online is a super important detail that I can't forget to handle. Because everyone who recommended a friend and every recommendation who received a quotation deserves to see the awesome result of our joint efforts to make the transition into the foster system a little easier for local kids.

I'm sure that a lot of our success with the campaign is due to Vince's new script and the role-playing the staff has been doing in meetings. Almost as soon as we began, the recommendations had really begun to flow. And the after-effects of volunteering aren't to be underestimated – they had kept the team's motivation and spirits high throughout that last week or two, and even into this month.

Picking up my phone, I send a text to Vince: '52 recommendations last month, bro'!'

I get a quick response: 'That's freakin' awesome!'

'As always, thx for all the help.'

'How many recs from your business partners?'

I pause, perplexed.

'Not sure. Take care. Talk soon.'

Hmmm…This is now the second time Vince has mentioned something about business partners. I had kind of blown it off before, but maybe now that other things are running so smoothly, I should give it a little more thought. Could other companies actually be an untapped source of recommendations?

If other small business owners are anything like me, marketing is probably as much a thorn in their sides as it used to be in mine.

They'd probably be grateful for any help and exposure we could give them. It would be awesome to help out other local businesses if we could. So what types of local businesses would make good partners? I brainstorm, writing down all the categories of businesses that come to mind. Wow, just off the top of my head, I'd listed out 25, 26 types of small businesses whose proprietors would talk to people in need of insurance every single day. Not to mention, of course, the companies themselves. Yeah, this could be a real goldmine, if...

If I could figure out how to create relationships with them.

Unfortunately, I'm sorry to say networking isn't my strong suit. I can feel myself blush a little, remembering my fumbling attempts at it in the past. Sure, the common rationale is that insurance agents, or any salespeople, are naturally social animals. Not so much with me. Standing around pointlessly, drink-in-hand, desperately trying to find someone to talk to at a garden-variety networking event just isn't my style. Truth is, I'm a little on the shy side. Sure, when I'm talking business, I'm fine. But that's because the focus is entirely on the customer or prospect – I'm trying to find ways I can best help *them.*

You know, a leopard can't change its spots, Jimbo. If you want to turn other local businesses into *partners*, you'll have to focus on *helping them.* That's just who you are, buddy.

I suddenly realize that rationale actually falls into line with some reading I was doing involving persuasion – specifically the concept of *reciprocation.* Reciprocation is said to be one of the most effective methods of persuasion, and I'd thought at the time that the idea sounded like it complimented my personality very well.

Because the Law of Reciprocation says all I have to do is *give...* and ask for nothing in return...And let my business partners' desire to help us with recommendations and/or their own commercial business happen of their own volition, completely naturally, as an organic thing – if they feel moved to do so. No strings.

And why not? Isn't that essentially what we're doing with our Community Cause Program, community magazine and team volunteering initiatives? Just trying to do something good for the community and our customers. All of the positive things that are happening for the agency are simply a *by-product* of those services.

So we can refer our customers to other local businesses...but only to those businesses we feel are high quality, ethical enterprises. After working so diligently to create trust and loyalty, we certainly don't want to lead our clients astray. But in order to have a real impact on any business partners, we have to do more than just drop their names or pass out their business cards.

What else can we offer to these companies? Something of real value which will actually accomplish some effective marketing for them? And also make the program a truly practical, helpful resource for our customers? Our website! Just as the agency and our charity partners are featuring each other on our mutual websites, Wakefield can have a page of recommended businesses, complete with some basic information, logo, address and phone. Maybe even a link to each company's website. This provides a compelling value-added resource for our customers. Now I'm getting somewhere!

As my brainstorming progresses, I create an Action Plan and work on it off and on throughout the month, quietly researching and developing my program.

First, I spend some time checking out other business directories for our area, such as Angie's List, but find one problem – most of them are simply too big. Although popular with people, they all contain categories *crammed* with different businesses. Need a plumber? There might be 10 or 12 to choose from. Someone to do home repairs? Good luck sifting through the 17 listings.

No, our program would have to be a little more helpful and user-friendly. Like the concierge in a fine hotel, I want to provide a valuable resource for my customers by pointing them toward a small handful of suitable local businesses when they have a need.

Hey, that's a perfect name for the new enterprise: *Concierge Program*. As I visualize it, creating the program will be a team effort. We'll carefully select a limited number of businesses for each category, and vet them well. All team members will participate by helping to bring in partner businesses we can feel good about recommending to our customers.

I call my graphic designer and have her make up a chart so we can track each employee's progress, containing the types of businesses we will seek out and spaces to write in the business partners we secure for the program so we can track each team member's progress.

I decide to turn the whole thing into a Treasure Hunt, with the goal being for each of us to find one partner in each category. And I'll offer up a fun, silly prize each time they bring in a viable new partner.

After an employee has filled all of their business categories, the agency will treat them to a nice dinner out with their significant other. That's always a good motivator! And knowing these guys, they'll probably fire up a little friendly competition and have some fun with it.

Once again I marvel at the strong camaraderie that has been developing over the last couple of months. Yes, this'll be another fun project for them to enjoy together, no doubt riddled with liberal doses of good-spirited heckling!

Working closely with my website developer, we come up with a killer presentation for each business partner, whereby they will each have an *entire page* dedicated to their company on the Wakefield website.

The pages will have a photo of the owner/manager, a synopsis of what they specialize in, all contact information and a link to their own company's website.

As happy as I am with the way the Concierge Program is shaping up, I still feel that I have to find that one distinctive 'thing'. That special *something* that will make other businesses want to bang down our door to become affiliated with our agency.

A hook.

Finally, the pièce de résistance of the whole project comes to me one day after work when I'm aimlessly sorting through the day's mail at home. Included is an advertising/coupon book for local businesses.

I'd looked into putting an ad in one of these a while back, and at $200, the price wasn't all that bad. But I just hadn't been sure it would pay off.

And like a flash, an idea pops into my head – Wakefield's community magazine!

We can put ads for our business partners in our monthly magazine!

An expensive-looking, full-color display ad in a cool community magazine that is sent out to over 1,000 customers and prospects should be a pretty darn attractive incentive to encourage other small businesses to participate in our program. I mean, opportunities like that don't come along every day.

And we'll charge them how much?

ZERO.

It all loops back to the Law of Reciprocation, baby. *Give*...and ask for *nothing* in return.

Talk about a value-added service! What company *wouldn't* want to partner with us? They'd have to be crazy!

As Cindy walks into the kitchen, I'm giggling like a loon. Grabbing her in a bear hug, I kiss her soundly. As I take her in my arms and dance her around the room, I explain my "eureka" moment. Soon we're both laughing, her excitement nearly matching my own.

With that last piece of the puzzle in place, I'm almost ready to introduce the team to our exciting new Concierge Program. But first, I want to do a test run. That'll help me determine what to include when I write their script, as well as what possible objections team members may have to overcome.

I call my new commercial customer, Marcus, at his gym and set an appointment to go visit with him the following day at 4:30.

The next afternoon, I abruptly walk out of the office at 4:00, leaving everyone to wonder what my mysterious mission could possibly be about.

They know I've been working hard on something, but I've been uncharacteristically tight-lipped about it. Whenever anyone asks what I'm up to, I either give some vague non-answer or smile enigmatically and say, "You'll see." I know they're dying to know what's up, and I love building their anticipation.

Marcus is already a client, albeit a new one, so I think the relationship is still fresh enough to provide some valuable feedback I can use with the team when approaching other possible business partners. I take along an agency logo folder stuffed with the past two issues of our community magazine and a few items the graphic designer has worked up for me:

1. Concierge Program Fact Sheet

2. Mock-up of what a business partner's dedicated page would look like on the Wakefield website

3. Mock-up of a business partner's ad in the magazine

It only takes me a matter of minutes to explain the concept of the Concierge Program to Marcus. Using the materials I brought along as illustrations, I believe I make a pretty effective pitch. When I'm done, I sit back and wait for his reaction. After a few moments, Marcus says, "And...what's the catch?"

"No catch."

"But this is...*valuable* stuff you're offering here, Jim. And I love the idea, but I'm not naïve. Somehow, someway, I'm going to have to pay for it. So just give me the bottom line."

"Marcus, you pay nothing because the Concierge Program is a *resource* we're developing for our customers. It costs us very little to do, and in our role as their trusted advisor, we want to be able to provide them with recommendations of other businesses in the area that they can trust.

"I vetted you with the Better Business Bureau, I checked out your online reviews. And I trust my own instincts. I know that you're an ethical businessman who gives good value and conscientious customer service.

"Becoming one of Wakefield Insurance's business partners costs you *nothing* because we trust you to treat our customers right. And really, shouldn't we all be helping each other out? It's the right thing to do – just one more step in helping to build a stronger community." Marcus' eyes light up and a huge smile spreads across his face.

"Well, alright, then! What're we waiting for? Let's get started!"

That night, Cindy and I work together preparing the script the staff will use to approach potential partners. First thing the next morning, I present the Concierge Program to my team, using the same materials I used with Marcus.

"Jim, this is one of the most innovative ideas I've seen in a long time," says Paul.

Lou adds, "I think our customers will see it as a real value-added service. You can bet nobody else out there is doing *anything* like this."

"Hey, if it will help us to land some commercial clients, this could be a *giant* step in growing our agency," points out Mel.

Just as Marcus had, Lou says, "What're we waiting for? How do we get started?"

After explaining the Treasure Hunt and showing the team chart, Mindy pipes up, "Hey Boss, can I help out with this, too, even though I'm customer service?"

"You bet, Mindy! You're a part of this team, too. See? There's a column here with your name on it!"

"Oh goody – cause I'm gonna kick *all* your butts in this Treasure Hunt!"

With that gauntlet thrown into the ring, some loud but good-natured ribbing and competition ensues, with everyone making side bets as to who will bring in the first, and the last, business partner.

I tell the team that they each have three hours a week to devote to the project, with the goal being to bring a total of 20-25 business partners onboard by the end of the month so that we can launch the program on our website and in the magazine. I'm anxious to see the Concierge Program at work, providing value to our customers and business partners.

True to form, the group starts collaborating as a team immediately. A discussion progresses, spit-balling ideas on the best ways to seek out and approach target companies, pointing out various strengths each team member has, and calling dibs on specific businesses with which they already have a personal connection.

As I listen to them, it's clear to me that each member of the team is noticeably more engaged with the agency and with each other, working to make positive contributions to the whole. Every staff member obviously feels free to contribute their own great ideas, and is willing to take on additional tasks of their own volition.

And my own mindset has changed, as well. I no longer feel responsible for the whole kit-and-caboodle. More and more often lately, I find myself thinking of this as *our* agency instead of *my* agency; *our* customers. *Our* challenges, which we face head-on, as a team. It feels great.

Busy days are the norm now, but it's good busy. Rewarding busy. More importantly, productive busy.

Margie continues to stop in every few weeks with home baked goodies, usually bringing little Eddie along to see everyone. Our team enjoys any chance to shower them with love and support and it always feels like old home week when they come by. I continue to be heartened, seeing that the family is maintaining their spirits. The jury is still out on Eddie's condition, but he's a fighter, as are his parents.

Elizabeth brought over a fruit basket a couple of weeks after her campaign was over, and showed some adorable photos of foster kids receiving the backpacks our team stuffed themselves.

We have arranged to volunteer for Elizabeth again, once some of her new initiatives get underway – perhaps during a month when our worthy cause is a private family, and as such, there will be no organizational volunteering opportunity available.

And of course, our agency has a new cause to support, bringing with it new contacts, a new press release to write and place, another fun volunteer afternoon and a Cause Rally Day to prepare for and conduct.

Additionally, we have ongoing website and social media posts to strategize and place, and steadily growing recommendations to follow-up with, along with working steadily to secure reputable business partners in our Concierge Program Treasure Hunt.

Yeah, it's been a crazy month, alright. But it's a good crazy.

Even with everything going on, by the time October rolls around the team has added 23 business partners, and we're ready to introduce our new Concierge Program to our customers.

Don't you just love it when a plan comes together?

Several days later, I make an appointment to stop by and see Marcus. Driving through town on a gorgeous, crisp fall day, I'm feeling pretty pleased with the state of my world.

Arriving at the gym, I proudly show Marcus the beautiful, full-color ad we placed for him in the latest issue of Wakefield's community magazine. Marcus is speechless as I hand him a good handful of magazines to share with his own customers.

"Oh, and Marcus, before I forget – here's your bill for services rendered." I pass him an invoice describing in some detail the magazine advertisement and webpage we designed for his business.

At the bottom of the page in bright, bold red ink, it reads, 'Total Due: $0.00'. Marcus bursts out laughing.

"Man, you are too much, Jim! I can't thank you enough for this."

"Don't mention it, Marcus. It was my pleasure, truly!

The idea of the Concierge Program was developed long ago by AMM's Chairman, Jay Adkins, for use in his own highly-successful insurance agencies. Believing other small business owners to be an untapped market for recommendations, he refined the program over time to make it a powerhouse resource for customers and the primary source of referrals to his agency.

AMM handles the design of business partner ads for our clients' monthly *Our Hometown* magazine because we believe the Concierge Program to be another vital cog in an agency's marketing.

Paying it forward is a powerful concept. It's a concept Jim has been harnessing throughout his marketing efforts this year, without even realizing it – paying it forward with customers, with charity organizations and now, with other businesses.

How do you know which businesses to approach? You can start by checking out Angie's List and Yelp for great reviews of local companies. You can even ask your customers for recommendations of other businesses who have delivered exceptional service and value. It will get them engaged in the process and as we all know, customer engagement is a good thing.

Every single one of your customers utilizes other area small businesses, and as we've seen, consumers don't always know who they can trust. Sometimes they'll share their needs with you, especially if they dovetail with policies you've written for them.

But providing a fully-fleshed out resource for all manner of services customers may need, will take your previously simply-helpful referral, to whole other level.

It's the difference between providing your customers with good service vs. showering them with *exceptional* service.

A Concierge Program is part and parcel of becoming a trusted advisor in people's everyday lives and gives customers another reason to be loyal to your agency for the long-term.

The bottom line is that any local business with a focus on providing high-quality services has the potential to become a trusted partner in your agency's Concierge Program. Targeting those whose services intersect frequently with insurance products is a great place to begin your network.

Look first toward:

- Real Estate Professionals
- Mortgage Brokers
- Apartment Complexes
- Car Dealerships
- Attorneys
- CPAs

For a helpful checklist of businesses that are good candidates for your Concierge Program, visit www.AgentsOfChangebook.com/resources.

The Better Business Bureau has a very easy-to-use website where you can vet any potential business partners. And again, be sure to consult online reviewing sites, such as Angie's List and Yelp. While one bad or nasty review may mean nothing, multiple bad reviews should send up a red flag.

Our Concierge Program is based on the Law of Reciprocation, which says that if you do something of value for someone and ask for *nothing* in return, you may end up getting a whole heck of *a lot* in return.

Do you think Marcus now has a wholly positive perception of Jim Wakefield and of Wakefield Insurance? Of course.

And do you suppose Marcus is going to think of Wakefield Insurance the next time *anything* regarding insurance comes up with a customer, friend, family member or fellow business owner? *Absolutely*.

The Concierge Program gives Jim the ability to create relationships much more easily than the typical *business networking* route. Keep in mind, this is just the initial step in developing a trusting relationship with Marcus, and it must be continuously fostered so the initial momentum doesn't get lost.

In the long run, a Concierge Program will generate more commercial business for your agency, as well as promote greater retention of your future and existing commercial business accounts. You'll likely find that your business partners become your greatest source of recommendations. And the Law of Reciprocation is an *awesome* way to make it all happen.

Our good friend Jim is about to come up with a couple of innovations to his Concierge Program which will make it simple for his business partners to give him recommendations when they feel moved to do so, and will even raise more money for their community causes.

So, come on. Let's discover what Jim has up his sleeve next.

CHAPTER ELEVEN
LIGHTS, CAMERA, ACTION!

The next work day dawns with our Wakefield team chuckling as I relay Marcus' reaction to being presented with a bill for 'services rendered' in the amount of $0.

"Alrighty, guys. It looks like we have a viable program kicking off here. We want to make sure that we really nurture these businesses and stay in fairly close touch with them. I'd like you all to take point on the business partners you've brought in yourselves, and put reminders on your calendars to reach out to them at least once a month for a 'howdy' call or a quick visit. As their pages go live on our website, please send along a nice email with the link, so that they can see their pages themselves. I've created an email template that's saved to the server, so it'll only take you a minute to do." The team seems to be engaged, thankfully.

I add, "I've also drawn up a schedule of when each partner will be featured in our community magazine. How about if one week after emailing them with their links, we send another short email letting them know when their display ad will be going in. So mark your calendars for that, as well, and I'll get another template done for you. Then you can just plug in the appropriate month."

"Sounds great, Jim, but I've been thinking..."

"Uh-oh, Paul, that's *never* a good thing," quips Melissa.

"Yeah, yeah, yeah. But seriously, when I initially approached my businesses about the Concierge Program, most of them asked me what they could do for us in return."

"Me, too," says Lou.

"Yeah, Boss, I've had a few of those, too," says Mindy.

"I know guys. But I feel very strongly about asking for absolutely *nothing*. Well…that is…hmm…," I think for a moment. "At least not for *ourselves*. Here's an idea – what if, when they ask, we tell them they can access our website and make a contribution to our current worthy cause if they'd like to?"

Mel exclaims, "Yes! Because it will reinforce so many great things about us in their eyes, as well as raising more money for our charities! That's perfect, Jim." Enthusiastic murmurs of approval flow around the conference room.

"OK then, we're agreed. When our business partners ask us what they can do to show their appreciation, that's how we'll handle it. I think it's a win-win on all fronts.

"Listen team, we have one more thing to talk about. I got a call from Marcus on my way in this morning, and it seems that last night he was telling his brother all about the ad we put in our magazine, as well as the webpage we worked up for him. And his brother wants to get a quote for his own business insurance. Apparently, he owns a small construction company. Cool, right?

"So I was thinking. We need to make this process ridiculously easy for our business partners, because it's going to happen – hopefully, a *lot* – and we certainly want to encourage it! I said I'd call him later and talk him through filling out the recommendation form on our website for his brother. But what if we handled all that up front?"

"How?"

"Well, what if after sending the email with their webpage link, we pop in the next day, get on their computer with them, and personally *show* them their webpage – you know, walk through it with them. While on our website, we can mention our Community Program and review past and current causes. And let them see our Rewards Program, which is how we raise money for those causes through recommendations."

"Great idea," says Lou, adding, "But I think we have to be sure to not be too pushy about having them send us recommendations. We don't want to de-value our original good deed."

"I think that'll work," Baxter says, nodding his head in confirmation. "If we just show them how the process works, then we're being helpful and not overtly asking for recommendations."

"You know, Boss, if we really want to foster good relationships with our business partners, why don't we send a handwritten thank you note whenever they do submit a recommendation? That might be a nice touch."

"Beautiful, Mindy! How 'bout you check the stock on our Wakefield thank you notes and maybe order a couple more boxes. Let's make sure each of us has a box in our desks, ready to go."

I continue, "So, every edition of our magazine going forward will talk about the Concierge Program and will feature an advertisement for at least one business partner. And we'll send out an email blast introducing the program by the end of the week to our entire database of contacts.

"Last but not least, this team needs to start talking up our Concierge Program! Tell your friends, family, neighbors and every single customer and prospect you speak with. This is a value-added service we've set up for *their* benefit. Let's get people using it! And, hopefully, get a whole bunch of new business for our partners."

Over the next several weeks, little by little, we all notice that the phones are ringing more – and not just the service line, the *sales* line! Hallelujah! A few of our business partners submit recommendations every month, sometimes in multiples, and the number is steadily growing. Best of all, they're high-quality recommendations, *for which the agency hasn't had to spend a dime or lift a finger.*

Every time a recommendation comes in from a partner, the appropriate team member sends a thank you note. If the recommendation turns into a quote, an email or quick phone call lets the partner know that a $20 donation in their business' name has been made to Wakefield's current community cause. And when we're able to personally point a customer toward one of our

Concierge business partners, we reach out to the partner to give them a head's up.

Slowly but surely, it's becoming clear that the Concierge Program is going to be an unprecedented success if we consistently give it plenty of TLC. Our business partners have expressed appreciation across-the-board, and all seem impressed by the value we've brought to their businesses, at absolutely no cost to them.

The biggest reward…many of our customers are beginning to use our agency as a field guide to other local businesses. Which is helping to actualize our desire to be viewed as true trusted advisors – in more areas than simply insurance and financial services.

As I walk by Baxter's office one day, I hear him speaking with one of our customers, Julie Chadwicky. Julie is complaining about how her yard is looking like a jungle with overgrown plants and bushes that she doesn't have time to deal with. I slow down a little to see if Baxter uses the opportunity to bring up our Concierge Program member.

"You should put Kate and Scott on that!" Baxter chuckles as he attempts to put Julie's own 3 and 6 year-old kids to work on her landscaping. I step into the office.

"Hi, Julie, good to see you again!" We shake hands warmly.

"Excuse me for interrupting, but I overheard you mentioning your lawn. Just in case you don't think your kids wielding machetes wildly is a good idea…," we all laugh, "have you heard about our Concierge Program?" Julie raises an eyebrow inquisitively and shakes her head. Baxter sits up straight and immediately takes the cue.

Having passed the baton, I nod and walk out of the office, leaving the two of them in front of Baxter's computer monitor, now angled so that Julie can see the Primo Landscaping page within our Concierge Program. Primo's isn't even one of the businesses that Baxter personally added, so I'm proud that he seems both familiar with it and comfortable talking about it. Almost there! A few gentle reminders here and there, and I know offering our Concierge Program will become second nature very soon.

Another interesting thing happened this month. A couple of sales producers from another agency called to see if we're looking to do any hiring, mentioning our Community Cause Program. Word-of-mouth is spreading about the positive activities our agency is engaging in, and people want to be part of it. Or they at least want to see if it can be a tool to make more money.

For once I'm actually building a reserve of experienced agents upon which to draw, without placing an ad or coming at it out of panic because someone gave notice or left. What a relief to be operating from a position of strength!

Now that I have confidence we can keep the customers we have and retain new customers over the long-term, I *do* feel ready to expand our team. And given the new business coming in, it's immensely satisfying to know that we're on firm enough ground that the agency can support more high-quality team members.

As I review our steadily growing numbers from the previous month, I know I have to share the good news with the one person most responsible for this turn-around. Taking out my phone, I send Vince a text. 'I finally got what you were talking about with business recs! More than got it – I NAILED IT!! Thanks!'

Moments later, I receive a reply.

'Saw your email with the Concierge Program. Well done! Spotlight them on your FB page. They'll love you even more.'

'Gotcha. THANK YOU VINCE!'

'It was all you. Just pointed you in the right direction. Flying now. Why don't you and Cindy head west soon and we'll hit Napa?'

'That would be awesome.'

The way things are going, the thought of an actual vacation seems realistic instead of a pipe dream. I breathe a sigh of relief, and turn to my computer and click to the Wakefield Facebook page.

Out of curiosity, I decide to perform a little split test. First, I create a post for the real estate professional we are currently spotlighting with an ad in our magazine, entirely in text, with a link back to the magazine. I simultaneously create another post for the business, but this time instead of using all text, I use the large image of the ad we ran for them in the magazine with only a short sentence of text to link back to the Concierge page.

At the end of the week, I see that the post with the large image ends up reaching 244 people vs. only 62 for the post that was all text. That's quite a significant variation.

I'm a data guy, and although I had *thought* that any post using an image would be more effective, it was good to have some concrete *proof*. From now on, we'll concentrate on using mostly images as opposed to text.

That brings to mind something unfortunate we've been slowly discovering with our emails, with the website and even with social media: it's getting harder and harder to get people to actually *read* the things we want them to read.

Cindy and I have been discussing at length a new trend we've observed – with teenagers and their cell phones, and even with adults. Whereas in the past, everyone was always texting madly, fingers flying furiously, now it seems they mostly just sit and watch the screen.

More and more over the past months, we've noticed that people simply have their eyes glued to their screens, scrolling through video after video. Well that, and everyone seems like they're trying to outdo each other with funny videos of themselves, or cool photos. Selfies. Snapagram or whatever it's called.

Both Cindy and I feel like we're slowly gravitating toward the same trend, unable to get away from watching videos. For quite a while, we've been getting the majority of our news online, perusing articles on the homepage of our browsers. But now, it seems virtually impossible to get away from watching videos if we want to pursue a topic of interest and learn more about a story. Videos are simply *everywhere*.

Hmm... Does that say something significant about reaching out to our audience? Do we need to make the attempt to engage our customers through the medium of videos before we miss the boat? Time to go into research mode.

Some very interesting information is readily available. It seems that even social media channels which were previously static, such as Twitter and Instagram, are switching over to videos simply because videos are exploding in popularity with users. According to a report from Cisco, by 2019 online video will be responsible for 85% of our country's internet traffic. I search for some additional info about video and jot the stats onto my loyal whiteboard as I find them...and they come fast!

VIDEO STATS

VIDEO IN EMAIL	200-300% +CTR
VIDEO INCLUSION	64% MORE likely TO BUY
TRUST	+36%
EXECS PREF	59%
YOUTUBE REACHES	> ANY CABLE NETWORK
YOUTUBE GROWTH	> 50% 3 STRAIGHT YEARS

I sit back in my chair and whistle. As intimidating as it seems, if we don't figure out how to capitalize on this form of marketing, we will likely be left in the dust in just a couple of years. And it could be another tool for our agency to further develop relationships with our clients and community.

I mean, that's why we jumped on the email and social media bandwagons in the first place, right? Because we needed to reach people where they were spending time and in the ways they wanted to receive their information and now, video communication seems to be the preferred by many today. Geez, I'm the guy who thought social media was intimidating! Where do I even begin with videos? I send a quick text to Vince, asking him to call when he has a few minutes. Vince eventually replies that he'll call this evening.

After dinner with the family, during which Cindy and Kenzie entertain me with wild tales of Ken's exploits at soccer practice this afternoon, Vince calls.

"Hey, Vince, thanks for checking in!"

"No problem, good buddy. What's up?"

"Well, I've been checking out the viability of using videos in our marketing, because it seems like such a battle sometimes to get folks to read anything."

"Well, that's sure breakin' out of your comfort zone, huh?"

"That's putting it mildly. But I wanted to get some input from you. All my research says that video is the next wave in marketing. What do you think about it?"

"Do you remember the first rule of good marketing, from one of my favor? We talked about it quite awhile ago."

"Yeah, I think so. 'Don't be boring', right?"

"Bingo! Get the man a gold star! Video is anything *but* boring. I mean, even bad videos manage to achieve *some* interest. I do agree that it's the wave of the future, but it's also a wave that's already here. Companies who're riding that horse *right now* are way out-performing companies who haven't even bothered to saddle up."

I laugh. "Nice metaphor!"

"What can I say? OK, I only have a minute, so I'm just gonna spew some stuff at you.

"Think of video as another spoke in the wheel of a well-rounded marketing campaign. Different people want to be reached in different ways, through different mediums. The more mediums you're utilizing consistently to spread your message, the more people you'll reach, the more your brand will get out there, the more trust and loyalty you'll develop and the more business you'll have.

"Make sense?"

"Yeah, actually."

"Just keep in mind the 3 M's of marketing, Jimbo: message, market, media. And give yourself a chance. What you've accomplished already is incredible, and I'm proud of you. But this is no time to sit back and relax. Video could really help get you to the level of sustainability that I know you want for your agency.

"So go ahead and try writing some scripts. And Jim?"

"Yeah?"

"*Don't be boring!* OK, gotta go. Give my love to your ladies, and tell Kenzie I'm gonna *kill* her in croquet next time around and reclaim my title!"

"Will do. Thanks, man. Call when you get in and we'll have you out to burn some burgers. And, hey, you can *try* to beat my daughter in croquet. If you manage to do it, you'll have to let me know how – because she always kicks *my* butt!"

Cindy and I talk late into the evening about the video idea. As usual, my wife has some great ideas. We come up with a list of points we always seem to struggle to get across to our customers, and which I hope to more effectively convey through video...

1. The reasons many people go through needless financial hardship when bad things happen. My team and I are always preaching about this, but a video would not only standardize the message, it could be viewed more than once and even be passed along to benefit other people.

2. Not all agencies are created equal! Wakefield is doing things vastly differently from the other guys, and there are distinct benefits to being one of our customers:

- Community magazine
- Community Cause Program
- Agency contributions to worthy causes on their behalf
- Team volunteer activities
- Concierge Program

3. Explanation of policies. After all, they can be quite confusing to people who don't know about, and talk about, insurance every day.

The next morning, I take a stab at writing video scripts. I work on them for a couple of days, and when I'm fairly satisfied with them I start researching how to create the videos. I find an online resource for creating animated videos. That might fulfill part of the 'don't be boring' credo, and heaven knows *I* don't want to be in front of a camera!

After handing some of my regular responsibilities off to my team so that I can really focus on it for a couple of weeks, I wrestle around with it and finally manage to complete two videos. Keeping in mind what I've learned about most people's attention spans being short even when watching videos, I've kept them both short and sweet.

After screening the videos for everyone on the team, as well as for Cindy and Kenzie, it seems as if I've managed to get across the message I'd hoped. And the general consensus is that they even manage to be somewhat entertaining. Whew! What a project. I feel like I've climbed Mt. Everest and am more than a little bit proud of myself for stepping so far outside of my comfort zone.

Mindy and I work together to figure out how to create our own Wakefield Insurance YouTube channel, and we eventually get our videos uploaded. After that, our website guy embeds them onto our agency website. That way, we'll have double the exposure. Excellent.

Oops, almost missed a step – social media! Creating the videos has been waaay too much work to have only a handful of people see them! Mel volunteers to post the videos through our social media channels, bless her heart, and Paul modifies our agency processes to include the videos in all applicable steps.

When everything is done, we have a team huddle. As everyone high-fives each other, I surprise them with a chilled bottle of non-alcoholic sparkling 'wine'.

"OK, guys let's toast! We have now *'gone Hollywood'*!"

"Hear, hear," says Paul.

"Well, that's a pretty loose interpretation of going Hollywood, but hey, I'll drink to that," laughs Mel.

"So, Boss – what's up next for us?" asks Mindy.

"Next, I'm going to go have a nice little nap, maybe a small nervous breakdown, and let *you* guys run the shop for awhile!"

Laughing, we all carry our fine 'champagne' to our offices to get back to work.

There is just no getting around it – video is no fad and is most definitely here to stay. Now, if you're not comfortable with the idea, you're certainly not alone. Most people know absolutely nothing about writing scripts and producing videos.

That's why at AMM, we handle everything for our clients. We focus on keeping their agencies up-to-date with high-quality custom videos produced by the experts in our Video Production department. And we post their videos regularly to YouTube, social media, website, and even include them in email campaigns.

We know what you're thinking. Doing it on your own may seem like an overwhelming project. It may even sound crazy that an insurance agency owner should have to worry about producing videos. But if you don't want to get left in the dust by the agencies that *are* willing to go that extra mile, it's something you need to seriously consider getting involved with.

Jim figured out how to do it, and you can, too. After all, anything worth doing is worth a little blood, sweat and tears, right?

There's a great quote you've probably heard by an author named Neale Donald Walsch:

"Life begins at the end of your comfort zone."

Take it to heart. Shake things up. Jim has spent the better part of a year now pushing himself outside of his comfort zone –

sometimes painfully so. When we first met him, all he wanted to do was take care of his customers and sell insurance, remember? It's been a wild ride, but the strides he's made, which have affected all areas of his life little by little, have been undeniable.

Let's visit him one last time and see if it's all been worth it.

CHAPTER TWELVE
AGENTS OF CHANGE

I stand in the Wakefield lobby looking out at the freshly fallen snow. Behind me, my team is jubilantly putting the finishing touches on the office Christmas decorations. Since it's the end of the day, they're enjoying cookies, cakes and other delicious favorites everyone brought in to make it a festive occasion. I turn and watch them for a moment, smiling fondly.

My team has grown by two members over the last couple months. Since I was fortunate enough to be able to be picky, they share our values and fit seamlessly into the existing team. It feels almost as if they've always been here.

Cindy and I have been toying lately with the idea of opening another office in a nearby city in the spring, if things continue down the path we've been traveling. Paul actually lives over in that area, and I think he'll be ready to manage an office on his own pretty soon. Because, I'm happy to say, business is just that good. Good? It's great!

As the phone rings, I motion Mindy to stay where she is and grab it myself.

"Hello, Mr. Wakefield? My name is Brian Newsome. I'm a reporter with the local NBC affiliate, and I was wondering if I could arrange to come out and interview you sometime next week."

"Interview *me*? About what?"

"Well, I saw your story in the News-Gazette this summer about your Community Program, and have been keeping tabs on your press releases and everything you folks have been doing over there. Then I ran into Elizabeth Jones from 'Backpacks of Hope' at a fundraiser the other day, and she mentioned how your team had been back out volunteering for them again a few months *after* your campaign on her behalf had ended.

"That's inspiring stuff, Mr. Wakefield. I thought our viewers might like to hear about it."

"Well, that's very kind of you, Mr. Newsome! Would you like to come here and meet the team that has been behind all of this?"

"That would be terrific. How's Tuesday at 4:00?"

"We'll be here. Oh, and you'd better wear some loose pants."

"Why is that?"

"Because these guys will no doubt force-feed you 10 pounds of Christmas cookies!"

Laughing, we both hang up. Turning to the curious faces of my team, I tell them about the half of the conversation they weren't able to hear. Mayhem and good natured ribbing ensue, with more eggnog and cookies being rapturously consumed. Just as things are beginning to wind down, the Kingston family arrives with a beautifully decorated gingerbread house carried by Eddie himself.

"Look what we brought you! Mom and Dad and I all worked on it together!"

Margie and Kevin are actually smiling and not just trying to put on a happy face. The reason is evident – Eddie is clearly getting better. He's put on some weight, he has color in his face and his eyes are shining with excitement. I know their doctors recently gave them the best Christmas gift they could ever receive – Eddie's cancer is in remission. Hopefully, for good.

Margie says, "The gingerbread house is for our Wakefield team of angels, but we also heard you were collecting toys for kids in the oncology wing of the hospital and the cancer center, so we brought a few things to contribute." She hands several brightly-wrapped packages to Mindy and Paul.

I exclaim, "Wow, that's so generous guys! Thanks so much! Eddie, we're going to keep this special gingerbread house right here in the lobby so that everyone can admire it. That is, until we break for Christmas next week – and then we're all gonna pig out on it!"

Eddie laughs. "Sounds good, Mr. Wakefield. I've got something for Kenzie, too, but I'll wait 'til we see you guys on Christmas day."

"That's probably best – no need to tempt her shaky will-power! I know she picked something special out for you, too. So, guys, can you stay and have a glass of nog with us?"

"Next time," says Kevin. "We have a couple more stops to make, but we wanted to get this stuff to you today. We heard you were decorating, and we brought something for you all. To put on your tree."

From his coat pocket, Kevin reveals an exquisite silver angel ornament and reads out loud what they've had engraved on the back: 'To our Wakefield Angels. With love and thanks for a year filled with unexpected blessings, Kevin, Margie and Eddie.'

As we all blink back sudden tears from our eyes, Eddie pipes up, "Can I hang it on your tree, Mr. Wakefield?"

"You bet, buddy. Why don't you let Lou give you a boost?"

I grab Kevin and Margie in a bear hug. "Thanks, guys. You're the best."

"We don't know where we'd be today if it hadn't been for you kicking off the support of the community for us, Jim, and for the kindness of this very special team," says Margie. "Everyone here will always be family to us."

After more hugs and kisses all around, the staff gathers in the doorway to wave as the family drives off.

"Now I see why you guys are so attached to that family. What *awesome* people," says Jose, one of our new team members.

Mel says, "Yeah, they're something truly special. But you know...*everyone* we've helped with our community program has been that way. When I think of all the people we've met – the beautiful families, the people running these remarkable grassroots charities, all the other dedicated volunteers along the way, even our new business partners and their own teams – it's just incredible."

"And to think," reflects Paul, "only a year ago, we were in our own little world. Just keeping our heads down and working a j-o-b. And now, we're making a real difference. Building relationships."

"Yeah, it's been an awesome year, Boss," says Mindy.

"That it has, team. That it has. How about a toast to even better things next year? Because when Cindy and I get back from the first real vacation we've had in *years*, we'll be discussing some exciting plans I have for our future."

Paul and Mel try their best to get some details out of me. I finally give in just a bit, and tell them that I've had an epiphany on how to take our Concierge Program to another level, and also how to blow away our goals for financial products and workplace benefits next year. I keep to myself plans for the probable new branch office.

I finish off the day at my desk, and putting my phone on do-not-disturb, I'm able to put some of the final touches on my plans for the following year. I'm very excited to test these ideas out, and especially since I can do it without the having the possibility of going out of business darkly looming over me.

Tuesday afternoon as scheduled, Brian Newsome and his crew come out and are greeted warmly. The team proudly shows off our Community Program wall, which has a separate little area dedicated to each campaign, and contains numerous framed photos, thank you notes, and the News-Gazette article. They tell him as much as they can about the worthy causes we've supported, hoping to get a mention, and further exposure, for each organization in the TV spot.

I explain how our website, social media, email and text message campaigns all work hand-in-hand, revolving around raising money and exposure for our community causes.

I also show Brian our community magazine and give him a couple of back issues to take with him. It's pretty cool when he and guys on his crew ask to be put on the Wakefield mailing list so they can all receive future issues.

Lou even explains our Concierge Program, sharing some of the positive feedback we've received from customers and business partners alike.

I can tell Brian is impressed that the agency asks for nothing in return, and that every recommendation from a business partner which generates a quote garners an additional donation in the business' name.

Melissa shares the story of one new business partner last month who was *so* excited by the program that she immediately submitted 15 recommendations. Wakefield quoted every single person, and we ultimately made a $300 donation to the local food pantry in her company's name. She was thrilled, and even recommended a new concierge partner – a mortgage broker who has already started sending us recommendations.

It's all a fun walk down memory lane, as well as an opportunity for our new team members to hear about everything they'd missed.

When the cameraman gives the cue that he's begun recording, Joe opens the segment by speaking directly into the camera while standing outside our office doors.

"Today I'm out visiting Wakefield Insurance agency because, folks, this isn't your typical insurance agency. They're doing business differently, by taking it upon themselves to be true Agents of Change for our community."

Mindy and I raise our eyebrows and look at each other with big eyes.

"Agents," I begin to whisper, but Mindy finishes with a much louder whisper, "Of Change!", before I can get it all out.

We all slap each other's backs, laughing quietly and grinning from ear to ear. I only hope our reaction isn't captured on camera!

Leave it to someone outside of our team to clearly see all that we're doing within the community, and then sum it up perfectly with three simple words.

Before I even know it, Mindy posts a picture she took of the news crew to our social media pages, alerting customers and friends of the agency to watch the evening news.

Of course, she ends the post with...

#AgentsOfChange

After the interviews are completed, true to form, the team plies our visitors with plenty of nog and cookies.

It's been quite a year for Wakefield Insurance, hasn't it?

When we first met Jim last Thanksgiving, he was fighting furiously to keep his head above water – and was losing the battle. In fact, he was coming seriously close to drowning. Jim was a man with big dreams for his agency, his community and his family, which he was unable to bring to fruition simply because when someone is trying desperately just to survive, there is no time, energy or thought for anything else.

But with time, work, patience and commitment, Jim was able to turn things around. And it was really just a change of mindset, wasn't it? Instead of expending so much time and money on things that weren't working and never would, he channeled those resources into building something truly unique and special.

With help from his visionary mentor, over time Jim developed a complete marketing strategy where each single piece of the puzzle worked together synergistically.

Remember, there is no silver bullet. There is no magical, single marketing 'thing' that will be all you need to take your agency to the next level.

But here's the good news…Have you ever heard of the *Force Multiplier Effect*? The Force Multiplier Effect is actually a term used by our military. Remember 'Stormin' Norman'? General Norman Schwarzkopf, commander of our forces in the first Gulf War,

Operation Desert Storm, spoke eloquently of using this strategy in that operation.

The General said he had utilized a wide variety of techniques and tools in the missions – air support, intelligence, satellite communications, battleships, special ops, artillery, tanks, infantry and much more.

The fascinating takeaway is that he was unable to point to any *one* specific thing, which was the deciding factor, but said that it was the *entire combination of tactics, used consistently*, that led to accomplishing the missions.

As you've probably figured out by all you've learned traveling alongside Jim on his journey toward excellence, we at AMM believe the same thing.

Yes, you may be able to employ any single one of the strategies we've discussed here and experience some limited success. But if you are looking for true agency-changing, self-perpetuating and sustainable results – results that will last for the long-haul – then each of these tactics must be utilized together, consistently, and seamlessly to form that perfect winning puzzle.

Here's some even better news:

Jim is not a black swan. He is not an anomaly.

We've seen these tactics produce results thousands of times.

At AMM we implement all of these processes for our clients, and handle a tremendous number of activities for them every single month. Our most successful agencies have teams that utilize and entirely engage with these relationship, recommendation and retention building programs consistently.

Why *not* your agency? Because if you do and you fully commit to it, you *will* see the results. And you'll end up with a strong, thriving, self-sufficient agency that fulfills your dreams.

We hope this book has inspired you to take action *today*, and that you'll begin implementing each of the tools you've learned from watching Jim and his team.

You, too, can be *#AgentsOfChange.*

EPILOGUE

In October of 2013, Agency Marketing Machine (AMM) was born, and the unique marketing program that John, Jay and Natalia had painstakingly tested and proven within Jay's insurance agencies was finally made available to other agencies.

This came about only after extensive effort to make the processes much more efficient, so that the cost would be something that nearly any insurance agency could easily afford simply by re-evaluating their marketing budgets.

The objective was to spread our *#AgentsOfChange* movement across the country as fast as possible, and the more efficient our processes, the faster we could achieve significant growth.

Large or small, independent or captive, the concepts you've learned in this book *work*. And because of that, as of this first writing AMM client agencies have joined together to raise more than *$500,000* for individual local families and charities. And that's something of which we're tremendously proud.

They've done this by raising typically between $500 to $2,000 per cause. Not huge amounts, but they often prove to be quite significant, raised when funds or supplies are needed most. The agencies also provide hope to those they've helped, showing that others truly care about their well-being and the community at-large.

Are you ready to implement the activities detailed in these chapters? We hope so! We've made numerous resources available to help you accomplish them on your own, and will continue to do so at www.agentsofchangebook.com/resources.

If you would like assistance in becoming *#AgentsOfChange*, we would be happy to show you exactly how we can help to make it all happen for you. Many of the activities will be familiar to you, since you watched Jim learn and implement some of our tactics throughout the previous pages. Others will be new. But all will be uniquely layered to take your agency to a level of success and sustainability of which you have no doubt dreamed.

Schedule a complimentary web demo of the different Agency Marketing Machine Programs with us here: www.agencymarketingmachine.com.

We are only able to work with a limited number of agencies directly, so we will let you know prior to our meeting if openings are currently unavailable.

If you think your agency consistently proves that you are already AgentsOfChange, we'd welcome your addition to the family and would love to help you gain greater exposure so that you can let your community know you're superheroes!

Apply here for a free listing and access to *#AgentsOfChange* resources: www.agentsofchangemovement.org.

47060142R00099

Made in the USA
Middletown, DE
15 August 2017